THE FIBERARTS DESIGN BOOK II

From the Staff of
FIBERARTS Magazine

Edited by Jeane Hutchins

Lark Books
Asheville, North Carolina

Cover: Detail of KEYSTONE *by Rena Thompson*

Copyright © 1983 by Lark Books

First Edition
Published in 1983 by:
Lark Books, a division of Lark Communications Corporation
50 College Street
Asheville, North Carolina 28801

Printed in Singapore by:
Kok Wah Press Limited
Jurong Town, Singapore

Library of Congress Cataloging in Publication Data
Main entry under title:
The Fiberarts design book II.

   1. Textile crafts. 2. Fiberwork. I. Hutchins,
Jeane, 1947-   . II. Fiberarts. III. Title:
Fiberarts design book 2. IV. Title: Fiberarts design
book two.
TT699.F52   1983   746   82-84032
ISBN 0-937274-06-2
ISBN 0-937274-07-0 (pbk.)

CONTENTS

INTRODUCTION

It's 12:30 on a February afternoon in the unheated back room of the third floor at FIBERARTS. The first of four judges for this *Design Book II* arrives and turns on the small space heater, hoping it will work. The second judge, coddling a warm cup of coffee, arrives in a parka, hoping the heater will warm up the room quickly. The judging coordinator arrives with nine slide carousels precariously stacked under her chin. The fourth and last judge follows with another nine carousels and clicks on the slide projector which loudly gasps as it, too, tries to warm up.

We're entering our fourth week of judging. While we each tire of the darkness, the cold and discomfort of the folding auditorium chairs, we are also eager to begin the daily viewing, because each carousel is filled with slides of work we haven't yet seen. What fantastic work will we discover today?

We've all got other work to do, but other obligations fade away as the bare bulb hanging from the ceiling is extinguished, the projector clicks and "Entry 937" is announced. We again enter the magical world of contemporary fiber. The experience of viewing 7,000 slides and photographs excites all the emotions: there's the exhilarating beauty of a perfectly executed tapestry of flowers, the sheer joy of a beautiful quilt, the eerie presence of a twined fiber sculpture, the giddy humor of a stitched miniature.

Two years, nine months and 15,000 copies have passed since the first *FIBERARTS Design Book* was published. We knew there would be a *FIBERARTS Design Book II* on the day we received the press proofs of the first *Design Book*. We knew we had to do it again. Like all good experiences, we knew it would be different the second time around, but well worth the effort.

As with the first *Design Book*, we asked the 90,000 readers of FIBERARTS Magazine to

show us what they considered to be their best work done in the last three years. And, again, the entries poured in. In the three weeks leading up to the entry deadline, we were flooded with slides and photos. The Federal Express, Special Delivery and regular mail trucks all convened in the street daily, as their drivers hauled in bags of entries.

The floor around the receptionist's desk filled with manila envelopes, then boxes filled with manila envelopes, then boxes on top of boxes filled with manila envelopes. At the deadline, more than 900 artists had sent us their slides, 8 by 10 glossies, transparencies, bios, resumes, philosophical discourses and, with them, the hope that we would take as much care with their entries as they did making them. With the help of four people and one small computer, each entry was logged in. We were ready.

Judging other people's creations is never easy. It's not easy to judge a piece on the basis of slides and photos, to judge without the opportunity to talk with the creators about themselves and their work or to reject so many excellent pieces because of inadequate photo quality.

It was also difficult to make the "rules" for deciding which pieces were in and which were not. We tried to stick to three general criteria: aesthetic quality, technical expertise and an ambiguous concept of "innovation." We used a system of "yes," "no" and "maybe" to slowly reduce the 7,000 slides and photos to the 520 contained in this book. Some works were judged without anguish or debate. Others required up to twelve viewings before we could reach an agreement.

We asked questions of each other, we lobbied for works that we individually liked, and we challenged each other's aesthetic assumptions and technical expertise. Although each of us has a thorough knowledge of fiber techniques and contemporary work, our personal aesthetics and eccentricities made unanimity relatively rare. But after the judging was completed, we came out of that cold room still speaking to one another, and started getting excited about "the book."

During the judging we had no way of knowing whose work we were viewing. But we frequently recognized the work of a well-known fiber artist or of someone recently profiled in FIBERARTS Magazine. Occasionally, we were so overwhelmed by a piece that we ran downstairs to the computer to find out *who* did it. We found, later, that we had rejected the work of a few "famous" fiber artists. So be it. Most of the work in this book is not the work of the rich and famous, but that of an eclectic group of students, working artists, teachers and many serious dabblers. This diversity is largely responsible for our excitement and inspiration during the judging and production of this book.

The decision of how to arrange the works into chapters was a challenge nearly as difficult as the original judging process. Since many works could have fit comfortably into more than one chapter, we used our best judgement to determine just where a piece would be most appropriately displayed. The first two chapters, Abstract and Graphic, feature two-dimensional works, including the majority of weaving in the book. The third chapter focuses on Three Dimensions in a variety of techniques. The Miniatures chapter concentrates on small scale works of various techniques and the Wearables chapter is a potpourri of technical styles. The Stitched, Pressed, Knotted, Entwined chapter presents paper-making, felting, embroidery, knitting, stitchery and basketry. There are also chapters dedicated to Surface Design and Quilting, and the last chapter, Diversions, is an assortment of whimsy, eccentricity and individuality.

It would be presumptuous to make any grand pronouncements here about the

current state of the world of fiber, based on the contents of this book. We feel, though, that this book represents a more complete cross section of the current variety, excellence and vitality of work in fiber than can be found elsewhere. Judging from the works featured here, the level of aesthetic sophistication, technical excellence and clarity of statement has never been higher. Those who work in fiber today know what they have to say and are more comfortable with their media than ever before. What obviously makes fiber so special is the personal and physical involvement in the process of creating the individual pieces.

Now you're ready to begin the fun, so find a nice, comfortable spot. Turn the pages and share the beauty, creativity and love that flows from each work. You will quickly understand why we felt compelled to produce this book. The first *FIBERARTS Design Book* was dedicated to all the artists who submitted their work, whether or not it was accepted. The *FIBERARTS Design Book II* is dedicated to all of you who enjoy textiles. You are the people for whom we—artists and editors—all work. We do this for you . . . Share the joy . . .

The FIBERARTS Staff
Asheville, North Carolina
October, 1983

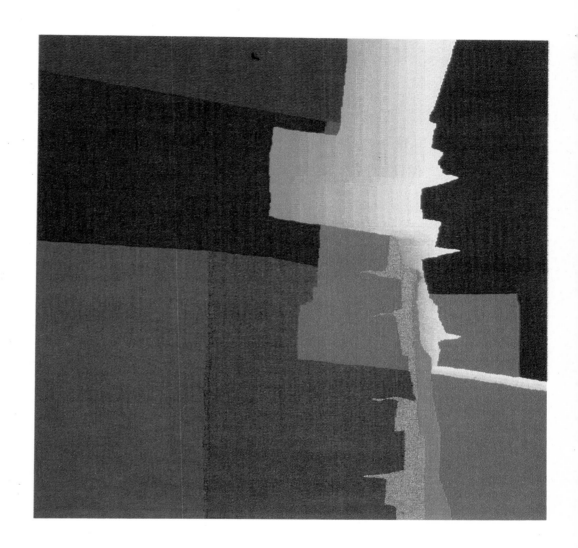

Anne Nearn Johnson
THE EDGE IN NIGHT
Woven tapestry (French
style); wool weft, cotton
seine warp; 5 by 5 feet.

A

B

C

D

A
Pamela Perry
AN OLD–FASHIONED
WALTZ
Woven, interlocking warp
and weft; hand dyed
cotton and linen,
metallics; 15 by 24
inches. Photo by David
Caras.

B
Monika Proulx
SEEN FROM ABOVE
Woven, high warp
weaving; cotton warp,
wool, cotton, flax, syn-
thetics and silk weft; 79
by 54 inches.

C
Barbara MacLeod
SHELL LANDSCAPE
Woven, stretched
tapestry (sculpted rya
technique); wool, lurex;
60 by 40 inches.

D
Carol S. Atleson
CREVICE
Woven, overshot and
inlay on eight harnesses;
cotton, wool, linen, syn-
thetics; 36 by 53 inches.

A
Connie Enzmann
SPRING THAW
Woven tapestry; wool,
mohair; 51 by 60 inches.

B
Connie Enzmann
EASTERN VIEW
Woven tapestry; wool,
mohair, cotton, silk; 48
by 60 inches.

A

B

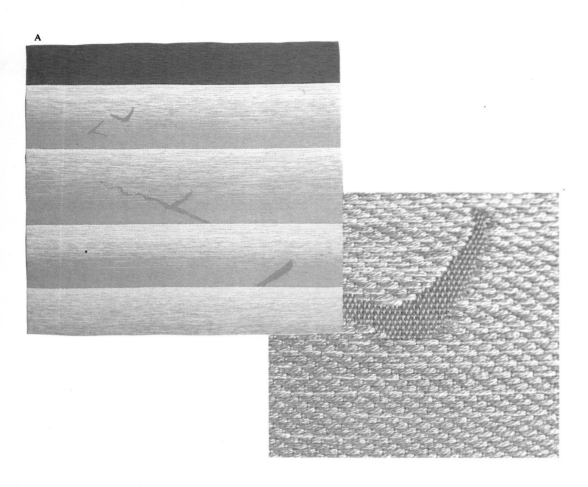

A

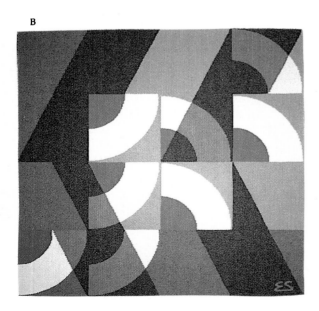

B

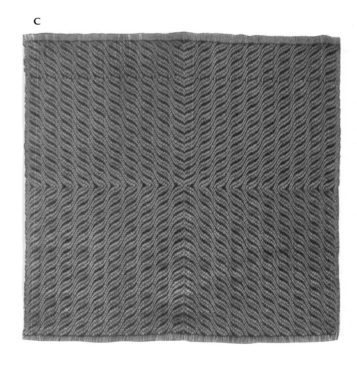

C

A
Barbara Setsu Pickett
LAPS/LAPSE
Woven tapestry, satin weave; Egyptian cotton; 36 by 36 inches.

B
Elinor Steele
CLOUD DANCE
Woven tapestry; wool, cotton, acrylic on cotton warp; 47½ by 46 inches.
I enjoy working with simple patterns that create a feeling of rhythm and dance.

C
Patricia Wheeler
WOVEN MANDALA
Woven, dyed and painted warp, twill pattern; wool; 17 by 17 inches.

A

A
Sharon Marcus
UNTITLED
Woven tapestry
(Gobelins technique);
wool weft, cotton warp;
42 by 54 inches.

*I deal with images which
convey my interest in stratig-
raphy, prehistory and the
ancient and fragmentary. I
found a great deal of pleasure
in earlier years in the excava-
tion of archaeological sites and
the discovery of mysterious
objects. I try to bring that
same excitement, that same
sense of seeing the known, yet
unknown, into my tapestries.*

B
Ann Newdigate Mills
EDINBURGH PERFORMANCE
Woven tapestry
(Gobelins technique);
cotton warp, linen,
cotton, wool and
horsehair weft; 36 by
29½ inches.

B

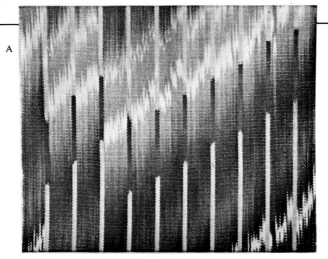

A
Nicole B. Mills
UNTITLED
Woven (kasuri technique); linen, rayon; 17 by 23 inches.

B
Claire Campbell Park
ASCENSION
Wrapped; re-bar, waxed cotton, wood dowels; 48 by 32½ inches.

I always sense the fundamental concerns of the spirit on the periphery of my consciousness but see them clearly only during rare moments. To do so, the layers of scintillating energy that surround me must be stopped. This series of work is about that energy and those moments of stillness and clarity.

C
Mary F. Donovan
BASIC MOTIVE
Woven tapestry; hand dyed wool weft, cotton warp; 32 by 52 inches.

D
Mary F. Donovan
MOVEMENT SERIES III
Woven tapestry; industrial and hand dyed cotton weft with natural cotton warp; 48 by 48 inches.

A
Sarah G. Vincent
CONCRETE SHIFTS
Woven, double ikat; noil
silks; 54 by 54 inches.

B
Joanne Soroka
WAKE
Woven tapestry; linen,
wool, cotton warp; 50 by
44 inches.

C
Sharon Phipps Kump
CONNECTIONS
Woven tapestry; hand
dyed wool, linen warp; 48
by 48 inches.

D
Judi Keen
GRADATED ORIGAMI
Woven; linen; 3 by 7 feet.

A

B
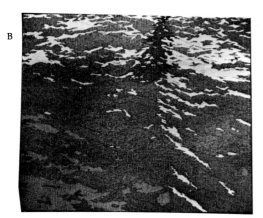

C

D

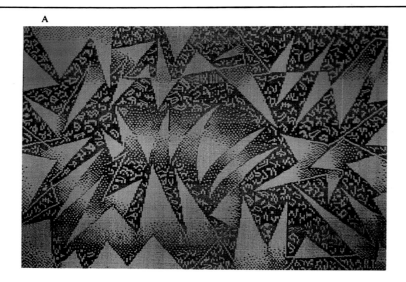

A

B

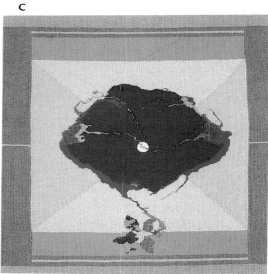

C

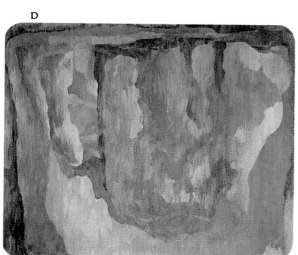

D

E

A
Rena Thompson
KEYSTONE
Woven, double weave
pick-up; hand dyed wool;
72 by 50 inches.

B
Marjorie Durko Puryear
SQUARES AND SPACES
SERIES #3: REDS
Double woven, stitched;
wool, silk, cotton, linen;
17 by 10 inches.

C
Elyse Coulson
RITES OF PASSAGE
Woven tapestry; linen
rug warp, wool weft;
22½ by 22½ inches.

D
Sherry Owens
RUNNING ON THE LAND
Woven, slit tapestry;
hand dyed wool on linen;
53½ by 45⅜ inches.

E
Gail Bent
ON OAK, THE MISTLETOE
Woven tapestry
(Gobelins technique);
wool weft, cotton warp;
48 by 60 inches.
*The tapestry has a Druidic
theme; the oak and mistletoe
being sacred plants (the title is
written in ancient Ogham
script at the top of the
tapestry). The pattern on the
ground is similar to that on
neolithic pottery found in
graves near the standing
stones.*

Militzer Bryant
GHT WINDOWS
e woven, broken
wool; 42 by 54

A

a Mender
LIGHT
; hand dyed wool
k, rayon embellish-
24 by 32 inches.

great appreciation for
imalists of the '70s.
LIGHT is meant to
e bands of changing
ggesting the illusion of
nt and filtered light.

. Gilfillan
EAVES LEAVING
tapestry, plain
wool weft, linen
50¾ by 32 inches.

C

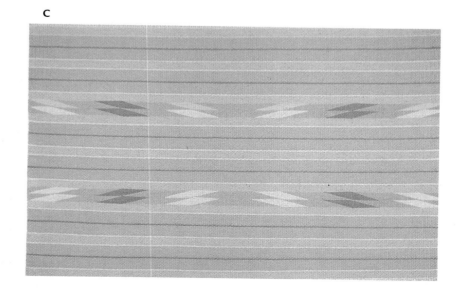

A

B

C

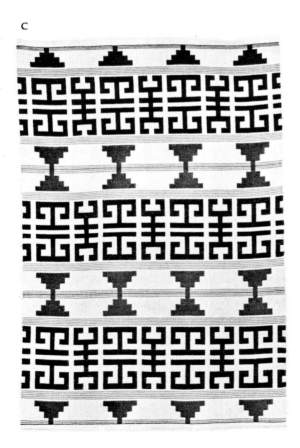

D

A
Teresa Archuleta-Sagel
RASPBERRY SALTILLO
Woven tapestry; hand dyed wool; 44 by 60 inches. Photo by Vincent A. Martinez.

B
Irene Yesley
INDIAN SUMMER
Woven tapestry; wool weft, linen warp; 48 by 60 inches. Photo by Michael Tincher.

INDIAN SUMMER *is a reflection of the influence the weaving and the landscape of New Mexico has had on my work.*

C
Margaret B. Windeknecht
ON THE SHOULDERS OF THE MOUNTAIN
Woven, loom controlled; wool on cotton and wool warp; 52 by 80 inches.

D
Valentin Gomez
UNTITLED
Woven tapestry; wool; 48 by 60 inches. Photo by A. Hawthorne.

A
Sherry Bennett
WARP IN SPACE II
Double woven; cotton; 24
by 24 inches.

*I use double weave to produce
black and white flat woven art
fabric, creating optical
illusions and movement.*

B
Harriet Quick
PAS DE DEUX
Knotted tapestry; cotton,
linen, wool, synthetics;
81 by 18 inches.

*I have been exploring the
possibilities of the half-hitch
knot for twelve years. There
seems to be no end to its versa-
tility as a sculptural and/or
linear element.*

A

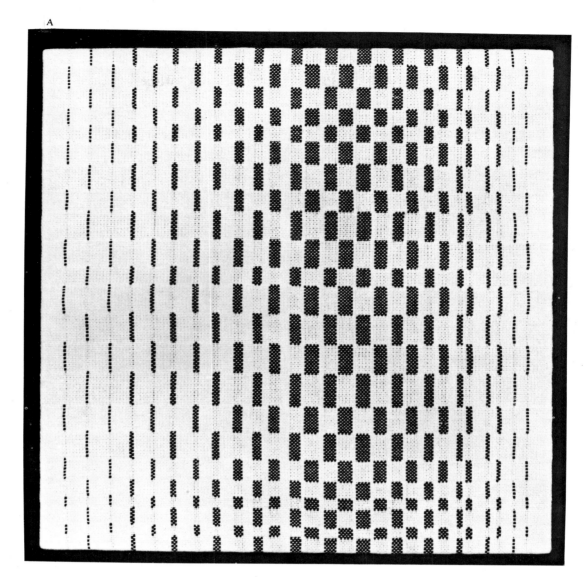

B

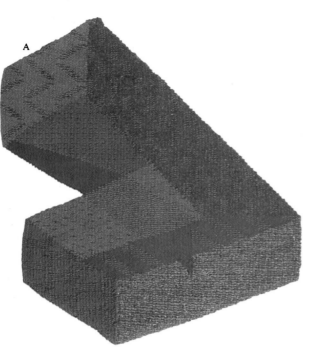

A

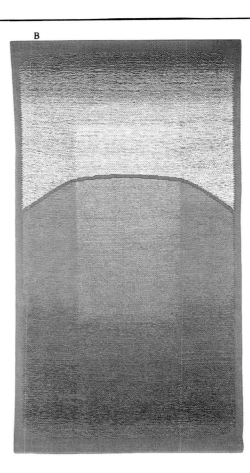

B

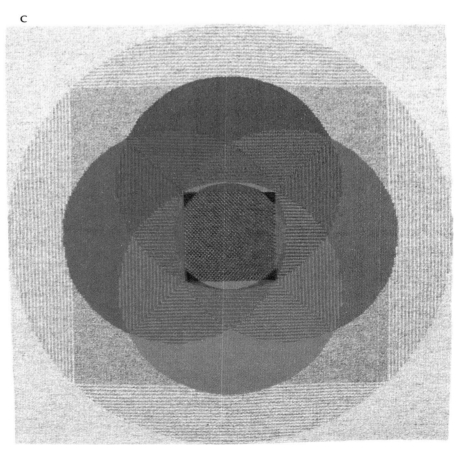

C

A
Barbara Schulman
QUILTMAKER'S MAZE
Woven tapestry; wo
by 25 inches. Photo
Jeannie Young.

B
Ursula Matrosovs
COPAN SILENCE
Woven, soumak tap
linen warp, wool,
synthetic and metal
weft; 6 by 8 feet. P
by Vida/Saltmarche

C
Carolyn Jongeward
ALCHEMY
Woven tapestry; co
warp, wool weft; 2
28 inches.

A

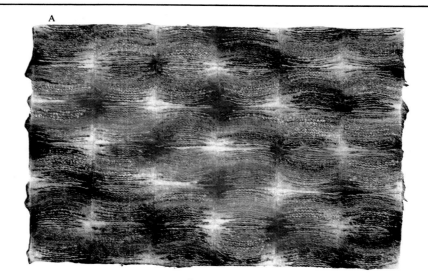

A
Fran Cutrell Rutkovsky
PLUM LINE-36
Woven tapestry; wool,
cotton, mohair, blends;
35 by 23 inches.

*The tapestry is constructed by
sewing together 36
individually woven tapestry
pieces in a pattern.*

B
Sally Bachman
SPIRIT TRAP
Woven tapestry; hand
dyed wool weft, linen
warp; 90 by 83 inches.
Photo by Robert Reck.

C
Sherry Owens
LINEAGE ONE
Woven, slit tapestry;
hand dyed wool on linen;
6 by 4 feet.

The elated stage of pregnancy!

B

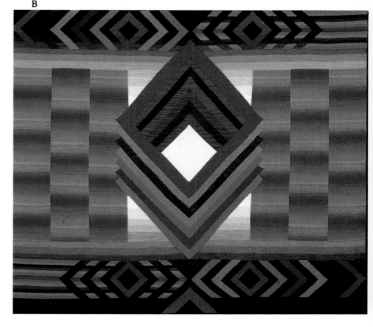

C

A

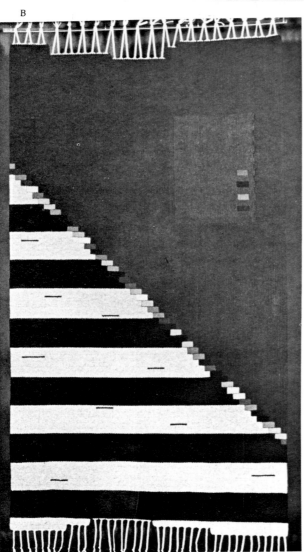

B

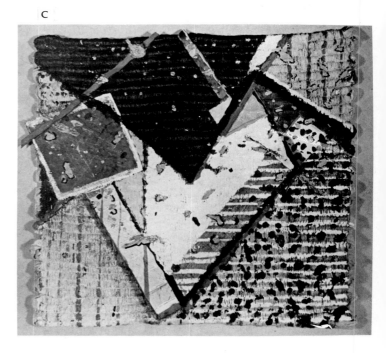

C

A
Sharon Marcus
PATTERNS AND
PARADIGMS
Woven tapestry
(Gobelins technique);
wool weft, cotton warp;
5 by 5 feet.

B
Nancy Shaw Cramer
EVERYDAY MEMORIES
Woven tapestry, inlaid;
linen warp, cotton weft;
47 by 87 inches. Photo by
Elton Pope-Lance.

*Designing geometric pro-
gressions in a classic
contemporary style, developed
for flat rugs, is the essence of
my work. For the past year, I
have been focusing on fragments; fragments of designs,
patterns, edges, color and
"visual erasures".*

C
Katherine Howe
SCARLET PIMPERNEL
SERIES: BOUTONNIERE
AND GRAY FOX
Woven mixed media,
collage on woven surface
with linen warp, canvas
weft; fabric, acrylic paint,
pencil, ribbon, color
cards; 18 by 18 inches.

A
David H. Kaye
ENGAGED INTERLOCK
Woven (own technique);
linen, hemp; 19½ by 18½
inches. Photo by David
H. Kaye.

B
David R. Mooney
PRIMARILY CONCERNED
Woven, triaxial weave;
wool, mounted on wood;
14 by 13 inches.

*In triaxial weave, three courses
of yarn intersect at 60 degrees
instead of a two-way 90 degree
intersection. In this work, I
am concerned with the three-
way interaction of primary
colors and with the primary
structure of weaving itself.*

C
Patti Mitchem
OSTINATA
Woven, warp rep weave;
cotton; 76 by 19 inches.

A

B

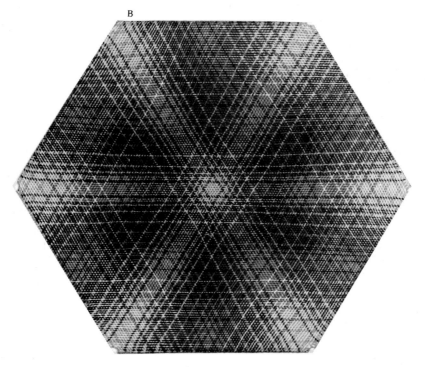

C

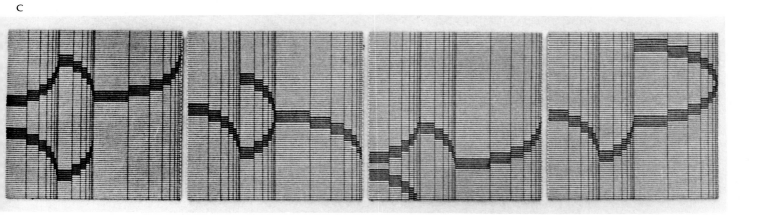

A

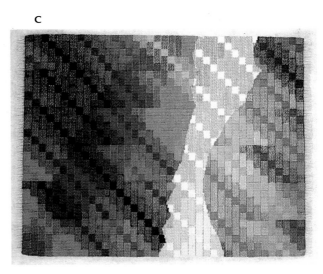

C

A
Arlyn Ende
UNTITLED
Hand tufted tapestry;
wool; 16 by 7 feet. Photo
by Bill LaFevor.

*This is one of 11 pieces
commissioned by Vanderbilt
Hospital (Nashville,
Tennessee) for the elevator
lobbies of 11 floors. Designed
by Arlyn Ende, hand tufted by
Paul Wieland Inc.*

B
Ann Watson
TAPESTRY RUG #3
Woven tapestry; wool on
linen warp; 40 by 61
inches.

C
Barbara J. Wyancko
MOUNTAINS AND
SHADOWS
Woven tapestry; wool,
silk and linen on felt; 29
by 24 inches.

D
Ruth Bright Mordy
PRAIRIE MINUET
Woven, tablet weaving;
cloth strips, cotton mop
cord; 21 by 3½ feet.

Martha Matthews
RAIN STORM
Woven tapestry; wool,
linen, cotton, polyester; 6
by 4 feet.

A

B

A
Jane Lowell LaRoque
BITS OF EARTH:
SNOWFENCES
Woven, ten-harness,
satin brocaded tapestry;
linen, wool, cotton,
rayon; 46 by 34 inches.

B
Jane Lowell LaRoque
BITS OF EARTH:
STONES IN WINTER
Woven, ten-harness satin
brocaded tapestry; linen,
cotton, wool, rayon;
three panels, total: 116
by 80 inches.

*In recent years, my eye has
focused rather near to the
earth, observing small places
that strike me as beautiful.
My work is realistic, almost
literal, but it is also sometimes abstract in appearance
because of this narrowly
focused examination.*

A

Martha Matthews
RAIN SQUALL OVER
BIG PINE KEY
Woven tapestry; wool,
linen, cotton; 58½ by
40½ inches.

B

Pat Kirby
VIRGINIA ROADSIDES #6-
AUTUMN GROUNDSCAPE
Woven tapestry; wool,
linen; 60 by 40 inches.

C

Pamela Topham
BRIDGEHAMPTON
MORAINE
Woven tapestry; wool,
cotton and linen warp; 46
by 60 inches.

*Most of my landscape
tapestries are inspired by the
waterways and farmland of the
Long Island (New York) South
Fork. They are endangered by
development of this fragile
area. Thus, I attempt to
"preserve" them through a
tapestry-record.*

A

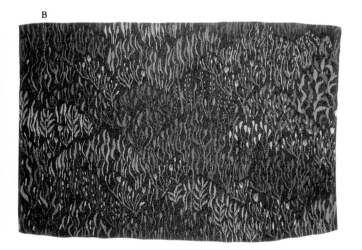

B

C

A

B

C

D

A
April D. May
WATERFALL
Woven; cotton, wool,
silk; 3½ by 6 feet.

I do one-of-a-kind commissions to suit the particular needs of my clients. The WATERFALL was designed to be a meditative piece to nourish a high-powered woman executive.

B
Lynn Murray
UNTITLED #1
Woven tapestry; linen
warp, wool weft; 8 by 5
feet.

C
Sarah D. Haskell
BEYOND THE BLUES
Woven tapestry; wool,
linen, metallics, rayon,
blends; 40 by 29 inches.

D
Shelley Socolofsky
LE LONGUE DE LA RIVIERE
Woven tapestry; wool,
alpaca, mohair, cotton; 33
by 24 inches.

I create impressionistic, figurative tapestry as a representation and communication of the "life vision". I select the images based upon my personal views of nature. By rendering nature impressionistically, I attempt to capture the peace and purity of the natural environment.

A
Dean Koga
VOLUNTEER PARK
CONSERVATORY, LILIES #1
Woven tapestry; linen,
wool; 17 by 20 inches.

B
Grete Schioler
IRIS
Woven, loom-controlled
tapestry; mixed fiber
yarns; 46 by 36 inches.

C
Molly Fowler
WHITING LANE
Double woven with
raised and felted figures;
wool, silk, cotton, ramie,
abaca pulp; 24 by 33 and
22½ by 30 inches.

*In this commissioned work, I
tried to interrelate the two
panels (order taking, selling,
receiving, paying); back and
forth between the two parts of
the whole.*

A

B

C

A

B

A

Ann Newdigate Mills
NATIONAL IDENTITY, BORDERS AND THE TIME FACTOR, OR, WEE MANNIE
Woven tapestry (Gobelins technique); cotton warp, linen, cotton, silk, wool and synthetic fiber weft; 43 by 39 inches.

B

Judy Branfman
COAST TO COAST: REFLECTIONS ON OCEAN PARK
Woven, warp and weft brocades, warp ikat; linen, cotton, wool, silk, mixed fibers; 64 by 58 inches.

I did several pieces on this theme using my grandmother as the central figure. The warp brocade adds another dimension to the surface and gives symbolic "clues" to the intended feeling.

A
Jaroslava Lialia Kuchma
HOUNDS
Woven tapestry; wool, cotton, acrylics; 4 by 6 feet.

B
Elene Gamache
SOIR DE FETE
Woven, high warp weaving; wool, rayon, cotton, metallized acrylic; 77 by 37 inches.

In my tapestries, my intention is to create a link of affinity between the subject and its medium. This medium is particularly evident in the representation of soft or flowing matters: fabric, living beings and granular substances. I want my tapestries to be a means of expressing my emotions. The subject and its medium must not be restrictive as such, but rather must serve to liberate my feelings freely and expressively.

A

B

A

B

C

A
Jaroslava Lialia Kuchma
SCHWARTZ
Woven tapestry; wool,
cotton, synthetics,
metallics; 6 by 4 feet.

B
Martha Matthews
OUR GANG
Woven tapestry; wool,
linen, cotton, handspun
human hair; 62 by 43
inches.

C
Susan Fletcher Guagliumi
EL COLOR ES LA CANCION
MEXICANA Y TODO EL
PUEBLO CANTA
Woven tapestry; wool
singles (three fold), linen
warp; 68 by 51 inches.

A
Michelle Morris
WOMAN'S WORK: MANHUNT!
Woven tapestry; wool; 48
by 36 inches.

B
Elene Gamache
PARADISE BEACH
Woven, high warp
weaving; wool, rayon,
cotton, metallized acrylic;
93 by 51 inches.

A

B

A

B

C

A
Elyse Coulson
THE DANCE
Woven tapestry; linen
rug warp, wool weft;
27¾ by 27¼ inches.

B
Alison Keenan
BLUE DANCERS
Woven tapestry; wool,
metallic thread, cotton;
21 by 35 inches.

C
Kristin Carlsen Rowley
FALSE FACADE
Woven tapestry; natural-
ly dyed wool on linen
warp; 64 by 39 inches.

*Of great significance for me
are buildings and walls. I am
drawn to them for their ability
to separate, divide, contain,
exclude and create space. A
search for meaningful building
forms led me to drawings in
an old book of Egyptian floor
plans and facades. They
intrigue me for their sense of
magic and time and my recent
work is based on these
drawings.*

A
Gail Bent
LABYRINTH
Woven tapestry
(Gobelins technique);
wool weft, cotton warp;
48 by 60 inches.

*The Latin words on the
tapestry translate: Lest It
Pierce The Soul.*

B
Rena Thompson
WESTERN LIGHT
Woven, double weave
pick-up; hand dyed wool;
76 by 54 inches.

A
Frances Penner-Ray
RINGS OF SATURN
Woven tapestry; wool; 36
by 21 inches.

B
Barbara Heller
ALL THE DIAMONDS
Woven tapestry; linen
warp, wool, cotton and
rayon weft; 7 by 4 feet.

C
Barbara Heller
THE CLEARING
Woven, hand dyed
tapestry; linen warp,
wool and rayon weft; 9
by 6 feet.
*A magical moment at 5 AM
- the sunlight just peeking into
the sacred grove of the goddess
- I started out to break up a
cat fight and ended by rushing
for the camera. I try to create
a quiet space in my tapestries
where the viewer can stop to
meditate and gather strength.*

A
Mary Lynn O'Shea
A PEONY FOR IRVING PENN
Woven slit tapestry;
wool, silk, rayon, linen,
mixed fibers; 52 by 60
inches.

B
Victor Jacoby
THE WIND IN OUR GARDEN
Woven, Aubusson
tapestry; cotton warp,
wool weft; 46 by 35
inches.

A

B

A

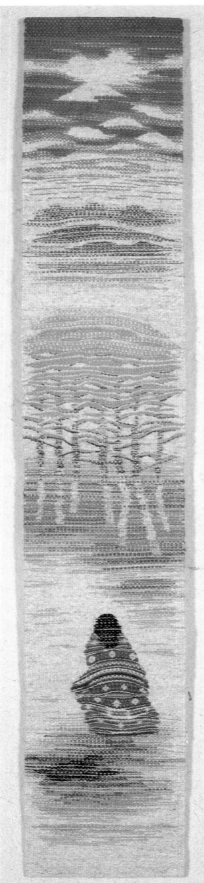

B

A
Carolyn Jongeward
WAITING
Woven tapestry; cotton warp, wool weft; 8 by 45 inches.

In 1978, I began weaving what I call "story belts". These long, narrow tapestries are woven spontaneously, designed in the moment of weaving. I sit down to weave, wait, then conjure design into being. WAITING, a conjured tapestry, is guided by the concept of waiting; waiting for the right idea, the right mind, the right thread, then weaving.

B
Yvonne Racine
FISHERFOLK
Woven tapestry; cotton warp, wool weft; 13 by 31 inches.

C
Inge Norgaard
MOTHER AND CHILD
Flatwoven; wool; 23 by 36½ inches.

C

A
Pam Patrie
ANIMATION KITES
Woven tapestry; cotton
warp, wool weft; 6 by 4
feet.

B
Pam Patrie
ANIMATION #1
Woven tapestry; wool
weft, cotton warp; 48 by
48 inches.

A

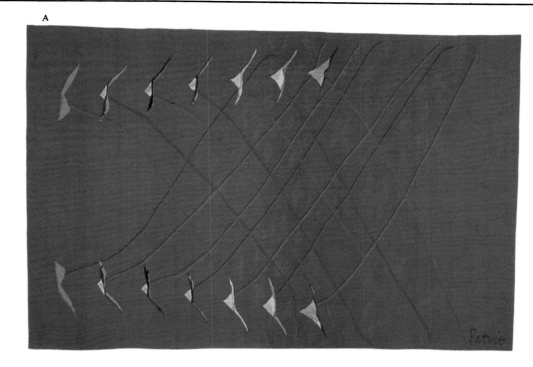

B

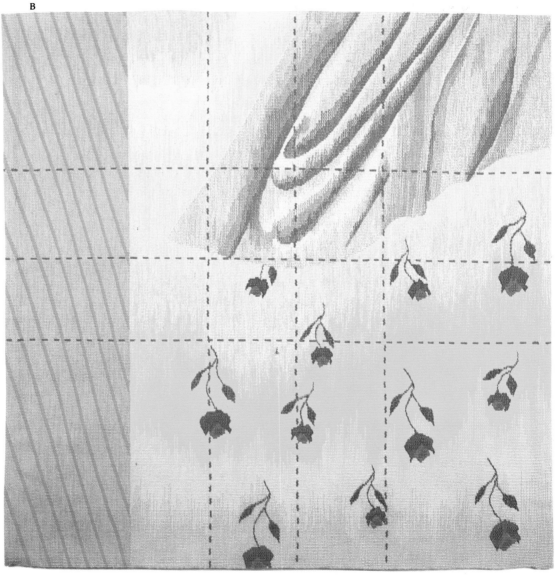

A

B

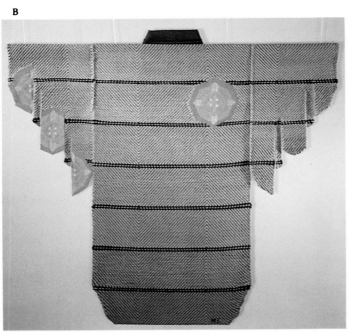

C

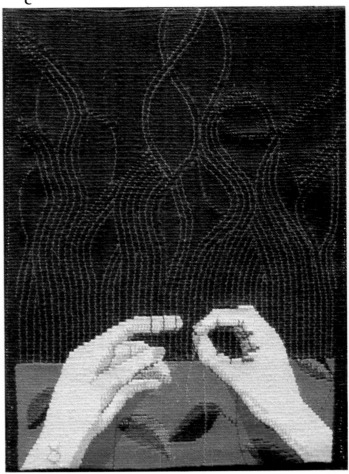

A

Patricia Bender
SEA ORCHID
Woven tapestry; hand-
spun and dyed wool, silk;
36 by 36 inches.

B

Pati Espenlaub
STAINED GLASS KIMONO
Woven, twill weave body
and tapestry techniques
on medallion, embroidery
on collar; wool, silk, pearl
cotton, polyester satin;
54 by 48 inches.
STAINED GLASS KIMONO
*is not a wearable; it is
intended as a wall ornamenta-
tion only.*

C

Jennifer Bennett
PAST, PRESENT, FUTURE
Woven tapestry; cotton
warp, wool weft; 12 by
19 inches.

A

Marcel Marois
PROGRESSIVE TENSION
Woven tapestry, high
warp; natural wool, linen;
124 by 72 inches. Photo
by Yves Martin.

B

Dean Johns
SONS FATHERS
Woven, high warp
tapestry (slit tapestry
technique); wool; 42 by
30 inches. Photo by
Kevin Kennedy.

C

Deann Joy Rubin
LE JEU (THE GAME),
MOVE ONE, TWO AND
THREE
Woven tapestry; cotton
warp, wool and cowhair
weft; 21, 22 and 23 by 50
inches.

A

B

C

A

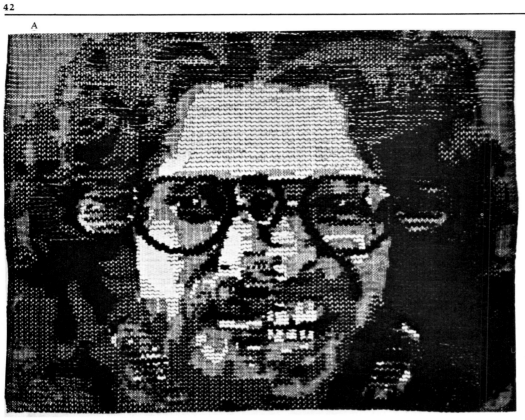

A
David R. Mooney
POLARIZED BROTHER
Flat woven, modified
Coptic weave; wool,
linen; 23 by 18 inches.

*Two photographs, taken
seconds apart, revealed the
serious and silly sides of my
brother, Mark. The identical
lighting and posture in these
photographs suggested this
polarized version.*

B
Penny J. Rupley
CITIES
Woven; wool; 108 by 90
inches.

B

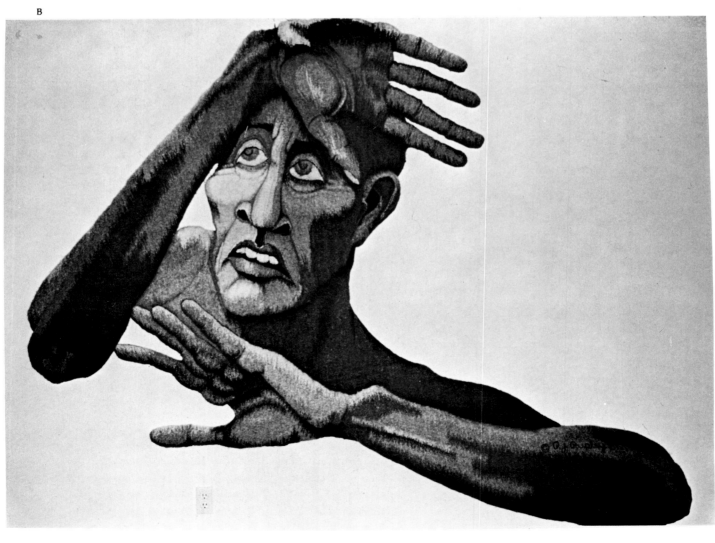

A

Dean Johns
FAMILY PORTRAIT
Woven, high warp
tapestry (slit tapestry
technique); wool, linen;
47 by 35 inches. Photo by
Kevin Kennedy.

*Most of my work involves
images of the figure. My
images are not meant to be
realistic portraits but figurative interpretations of the
human form.*

B

Zofia Dlugopolska
PORTRAIT III
Woven tapestry; wool on
cotton warp; 31 by 36
inches.

C

Carol Ventura
SELF PORTRAIT
Tapestry crochet; acrylic
carpet yarn supported by
a steel bar on top; 4 by 7
feet. Photo by Carol
Ventura.

D

Deann Joy Rubin
JEUNE FILLE (LITTLE GIRL)
Woven tapestry; pearl
cotton warp, wool and
cowhair weft; 36 by 40
inches.

*The design is from a slide I
took while at the Tuilleries
Garden in Paris, France.*

A

B

C

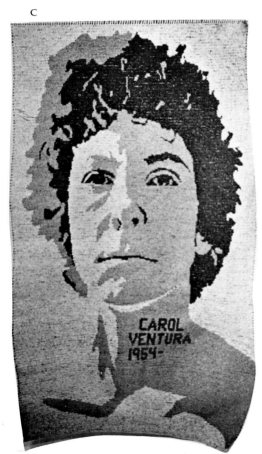

D

A

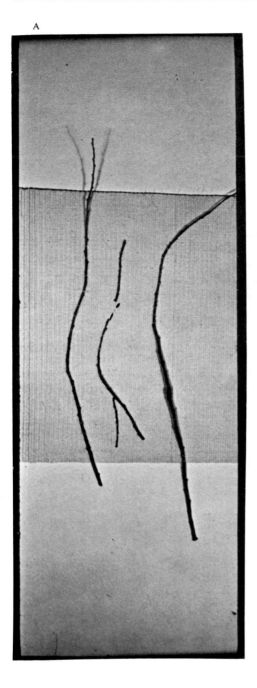

B

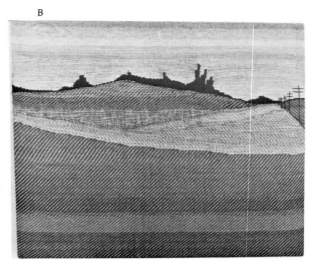

C

D

A
Marjorie J. Rubin
TORSO
Woven with sticks, stitched; linen; 12 by 16 inches.

B
Elaine Clarfield-Gitalis
NORTH DAKOTA
Woven, twill weaving; wool warp and weft; 52 by 44 inches.

C
Anne G. Clark
GREENER PASTURES
Woven, high warp tapestry; wool, silk, cotton warp; 25½ by 26¼ inches.

D
Patti Handley
Jerrie Peters
FIELDS AND FOOTHILLS
Hooked tapestry, cut and sculpted with sheep shears; wool, cotton backing; 156 by 54 inches.

This piece is one of five works commissioned for the new Federal Land Bank building in Merced, California. All pieces have agribusiness themes.

A
Guy Lemieux
IN OBSEQUIO
Woven, high warp art
mural; wool; 84 by 59
inches. Photo by Claire
Morel.

*I'm now working on the rela-
tionship between space and
time; two omnipresent life
constituents. I use geometric
figures to divide the space
transposed on the tapestry. The
temporal division is repre-
sented by the different colors
from one space to the other.
Lines and geometrical figures
mark out portions of space and
remind the spectator that
nothing is left to chance.*

B
Alison Magilton
BACKWATER
Woven tapestry; wool
weft, cotton warp; 38 by
24 inches.

*In this work, I aimed at depicting
the transparency of the surface of
water with the three-
dimensionality of rocks above and
below the surface, while retaining
the character of woven tapestry.*

A

B

A

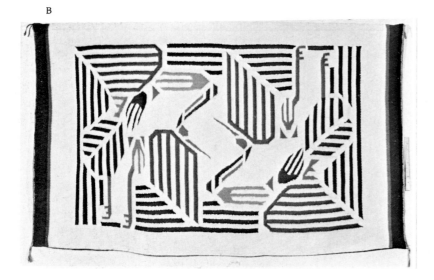

B

C

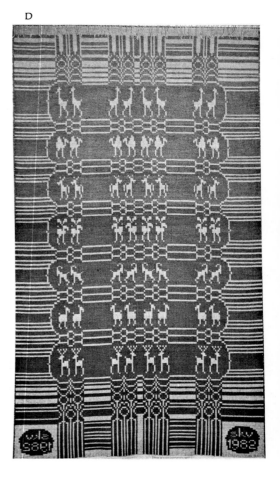

D

A
Renate F. Chernoff
ARK DOORS
Woven, tapestry technique; linen warp, linen, rayon and cottolin weft; 45 by 54 inches.

The design for ARK DOORS was inspired by the Talmudic quotation, "The world is based on three foundations - truth, justice and peace." Hebrew calligraphy spells out these words. The symbols used are the light of truth, the scales of justice and the dove of peace.

B
Cynthia H. Neely
CRANE DANCE
Woven tapestry; wool; 90 by 55 inches.

C
Mary Jane Miller
FANTASY
Woven tapestry; wool; 48 by 36 inches. Photo by A. Hawthorne.

D
Sharon Vandenack
ANIMAL FARM
Woven, summer/winter weave, 12-harness plus pick-up; hand dyed wool; 51 by 92 inches.

A
Jaroslava Lialia Kuchma
NAOMI
Woven tapestry; wool, cotton; 7 by 4 feet.

The design appealed to me. The woman is a dear friend and the influence of Matisse and a few Oriental masters needed an outlet.

B
Micala Sidore
TEPPER'S ON PLEASANT STREET
Woven tapestry; wool; 58 by 31½ inches. Photo by Edward T. Bissell.

This piece was commissioned by the owners of the Hotel Northampton in Northampton, Massachusetts, as part of their renovation of the building. The hotel reopened in 1982. "Tepper's", opened in 1940, was a chain of "five and dime" stores owned by three brothers which sold anything one might want. The store closed in 1982 and is shown here flanked by the Pleasant Street Theatre which opened in 1976 and the old post office which closed in 1976.

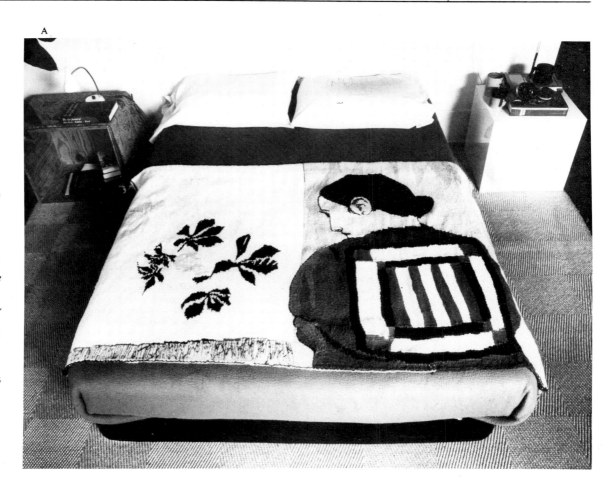

A

B

A

A
Dirk Holger
FOLIAGE
Woven (Aubusson tapestry); wool, silk, cotton; 45 by 64 inches.
My tapestry design work is entirely dedicated to lend harmony and warmth to modern architecture.

B
Louise Weaver Greene
CALIFORNIA SPRING
Woven tapestry; wool and synthetics on cotton warp; 48¼ by 23½ inches. Photo by Thomas Greene.

B

Janice Lessman-Moss
RHODODENDRON RAG
Wooden rods, porcelain
beads, pearl cotton, linen;
14 by 16 inches.

A

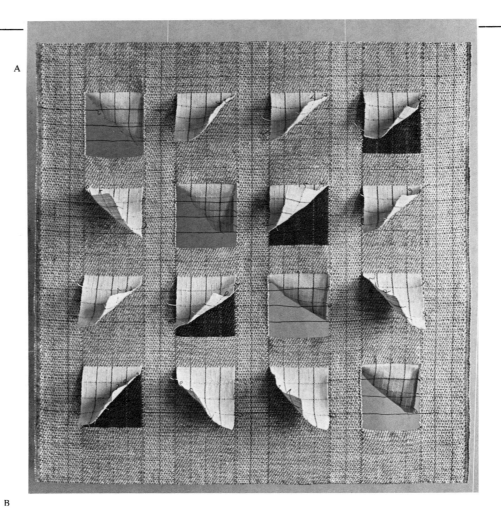

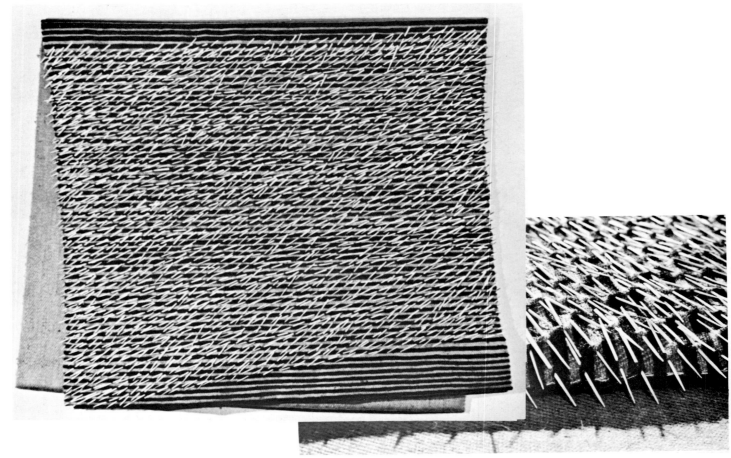

B

A
Tina Takayanagi Barnet
PINK X
Woven; mixed fibers, wire; 31 by 32 by 7 inches.

This panel is supported on a rigid, painted wire backing. Wire in the supplementary warp allows the flaps to be manipulated.

B
Anouk Stussi
AWARENESS
Painted; jute, acrylic paint, wood; 49 by 45 inches.

On acrylic painted textiles, as in this series, wooden elements superpose themselves, producing a dynamic effect by their direction, density, light and shadow.

A

Marla Mallett
BLACK AND WHITE SHIFT II
Woven; wool, rayon, synthetic; 41 by 50 by 2 inches. Photo by Marla Mallett.

My recent work is purely hedonistic with a concentration on the thick massing and interlacing of exquisite materials. My woven images are non-allusive; tactile sensation, color and the structure itself are the idea.

B

Linda Miller
INSIGHT
Woven linen construction (weft faced weave); 17 by 17 by 2½ inches.

C

Lyn Carter
UNTITLED #41
Painted, stuffed; polyester fiberfill and masonite stuffing; wooden dowel points, enamel paint; 46 by 46 by 4 inches.

Here, the soft flexible surface of fabric becomes a companion to the architectural structure of the piece. I wanted to bring "softness" and "hardness" into symbiosis so that one extreme might articulate the other.

A

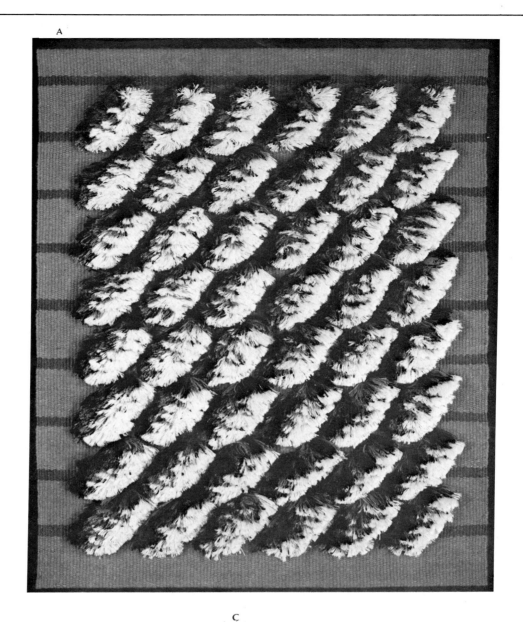

B

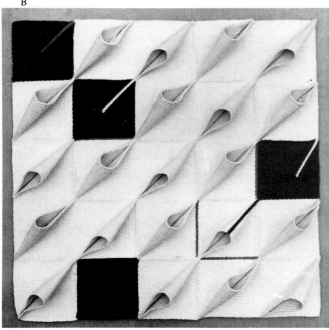

C

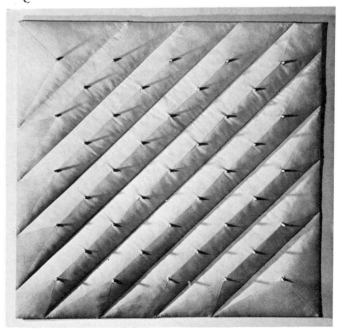

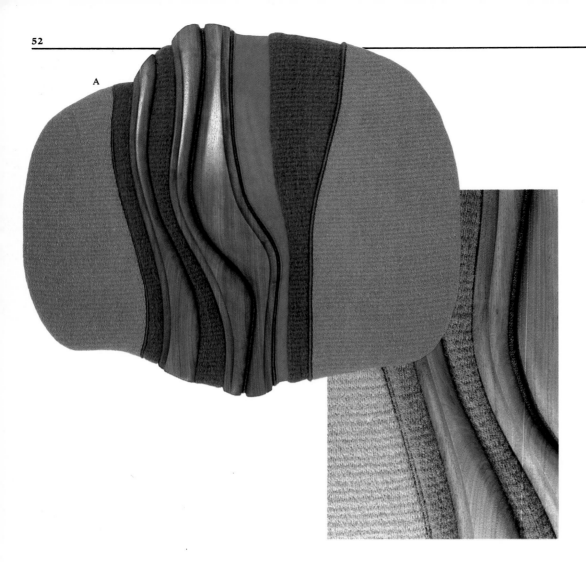

A

Grace Hamilton
MI FAMILIA
Woven tapestry pieces,
cut, stuffed and incor-
porated onto a shaped
plywood backing with
sculpted walnut and
suede; hand dyed wool;
30 by 26 by 2½ inches.

*This wall hanging represents
my family: my husband and I
and the product of our relationship, our daughter. It
represents the harmonious flow
of our lives together.*

B
Donna Braverman
TRIAD
Wrapped; linen, rayon,
floss, PVC tubing, plexi-
glass, wood; 72 by 24 by
11 inches. Photo by
Donna Braverman.

*My technique begins with
cylindrical tubes wrapped with
hand dyed natural fibers, then
combined to form larger geometrical modules. These forms
incorporate textures and colors
that create a subtle interplay of
light and shadow. Shadows
and negative spaces are just as
important as the structures
themselves. Mirrors on the
sides of each module provide a
floating, airy quality to the
sculptures while serving as
reflectional transitions from
module to module.*

B

A
Molly Hart
ECHAPEE
**Woven, weft face
tapestry; silk, linen,
rayon; 7 by 5 feet.**

*This piece was inspired by a
geological depiction of the
movement of earth waves. The
title is a musical term meaning
the escape tone, which also
suggests receding motion in
sound.*

B
Tammy Kulamer
OPEN WALL COLOR
PROGRESSION
**Woven, weft face
tapestry strips, plaited;
wool; 96 by 96 by 2½
inches.**

A

B

A

B

C

A
Cynthia Gale Nosek
THE BARON AT 25
Crocheted and stuffed
over armature wire;
wool, hair of mohair,
polyester stuffing; 23 by
21 by 14 inches.

B
Bonnie R. Hargrove
MEDICINE MAN'S
TURTLE RATTLE
Knotted; dyed cotton
thread, wood, seeds (for
rattle); 6 by 1½ by 2¼
inches (including handle).

*For a long time, I have felt a
kindred spirit with the
American Indian. This piece
was inspired by a childhood
book. By knotting in small
scale, I feel a strong bond with
my work.*

C
Andrea V. Uravitch
SPIRIT OF THE RENWICK
Woven, crocheted, carved
base; wool, cotton, glass
eyes, wooden and stryo-
foam base; 25 by 34 by
7½ inches. Photo by
Andrea V. Uravitch.

A
Jappie King Black
DEFACED BASKET
Crocheted, stitched, woven, wrapped, coiled, airbrush hand painted; linen, cotton, paper rush; 22 by 16 by 6 inches. Photo by Richard W. Black.

B
Jan Sousa
KNOTTING, BASKET, BLOOD
Handmade linen paper, knotted with raffia; antique Karok basket, blood; 14 by 17 by 3 inches.

This piece combines some old and new together. The unbleached linen is an antique from an old cloth, the basketry fragment is also old and the dentalia beads are from an old Sioux breastplate. It is watercolored in my own blood.

C
Dawn MacNutt
DAVID'S HEAD
Woven on loom, sculpted by hand, electroplated, oxidized; 20 gauge copper wire; 24 by 20 by 20 inches.

D
Marie McGill
WINTER SPIRIT
Needle woven face; all wool; 39 by 48 inches.

This is the winter spirit of flight. It has textured feather images and the face has a raised hood with hanging feather images surrounding it. White is my symbolic color for snow.

B

C

D

A

A
Gloria E. Crouse
RAZ–MA–TAZ
Woven (painted warp),
rug hooking techniques;
cotton, synthetics, velvet
tubing, bias cut taffetas,
torn twills; 72 by 66 by
1½ inches. Photo by
Roger Schreiber.

B
Gloria E. Crouse
DOOR MAT
Loom woven, knotted;
suede, cowhide, sisal,
metal washers, gaskets,
rods; 78 by 78 by 1½
inches.

B

A

Patricia T. Hetzler
RESURRECTION
Handmade cast paper;
cotton linters, hemp,
Procion and direct dyes,
cotton tapes, wrapped
plastic tubing, silk thread;
22 by 28 by 3 inches.

*I have always loved paper -
any kind, and I find it
enormously exciting to make
paper. As a medium, paper
has such a vast range of possibilities. One could never tire of
exploring its physical and
spiritual qualities.*

B

Marcia Waldman
LEMONADE DREAM
Woven, plain weave, ikat
dyed, hand stitched;
linen; 42 by 46 inches.

*My mood, thus my mode of
expression, is often directly
related to the changing seasons.
This is reflected in the way I
use color and form. Here, I
found freedom through an
immersion in movement and
blossoms of spring.*

C

Margaret Welty
ROPES X'S THREE
Hand plied, hand dyed;
cotton, rayon, silk, linen,
wool; 12 feet by 30 by 4
to 10 inches.

A

B

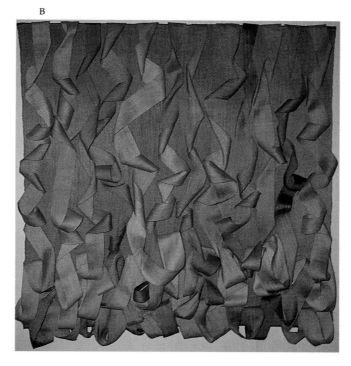

C

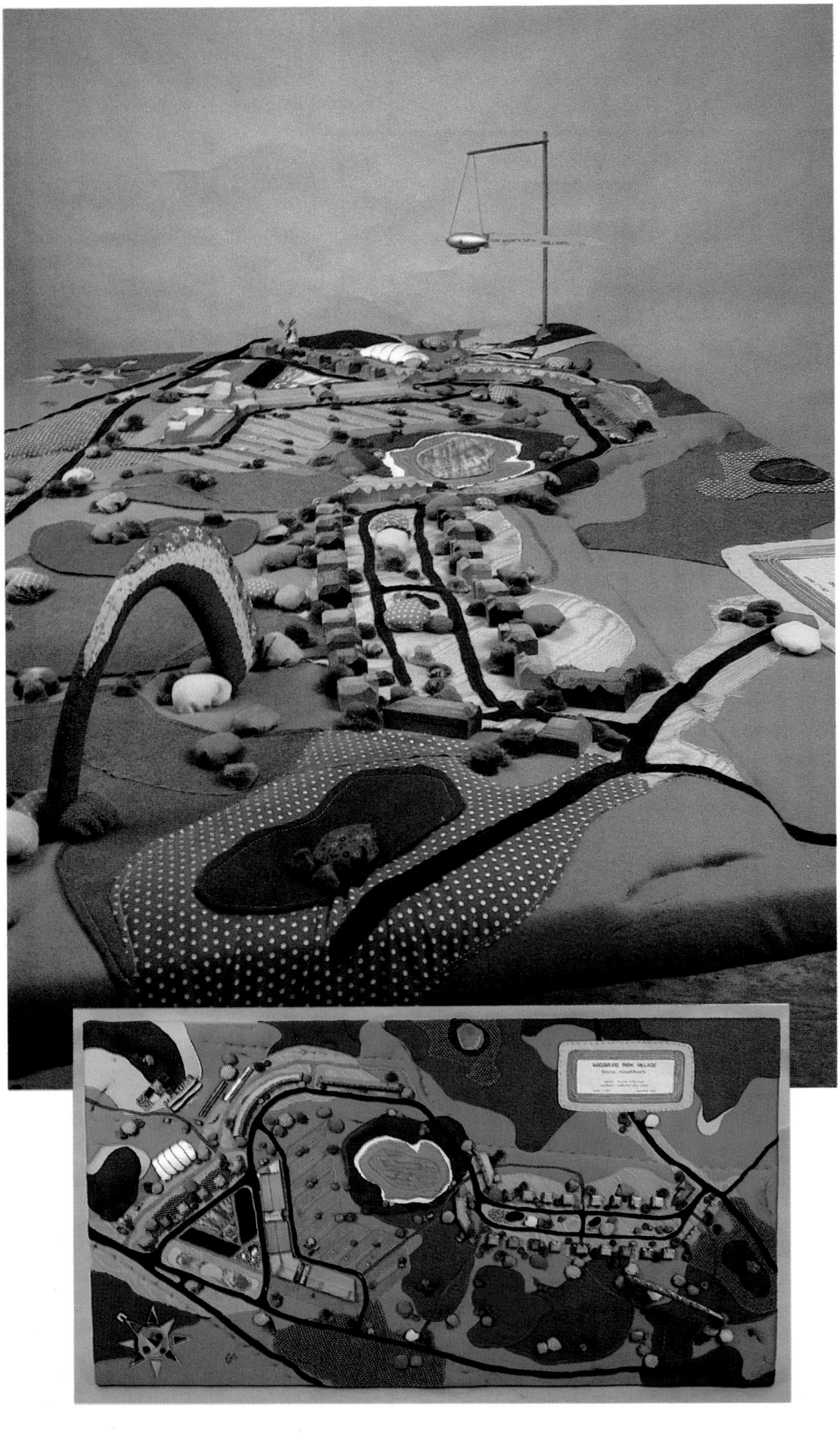

A

Pamela Martell
SOFT SCULPTURE
ARCHITECTURAL MODEL
(1″ = 50′)
Appliqued cover
stretched over plateaus
constructed from
topographical map of site;
cotton, wool, satin,
jersey, mylar, wood,
plastic; 48 by 72 by 8
inches.

*An architect familiar with my
wall murals asked me to translate my style onto a model of a
site plan for a professional
development. Faced with many
community hearings, she
wanted a presentation tool that
would be "upbeat, small,
appealing and less intimi-
dating" than the usual models.*

A
Barbara MacLeod
LEVI'S POCKET
Mountains are hand-
woven, pocket is denim
stretched over wood; 16
by 20 feet.

*This piece hangs in a very
large mall in Toronto,
Ontario, Canada, and was a
competition commission
sponsored by the Levi people.*

B
Hey Frey
John Guest
NORTH AMERICAN YURT
Handmade felt, wool,
wood, acrylic paint,
bamboo, rope and nails;
10 feet in diameter, 11
feet tall.

A

B

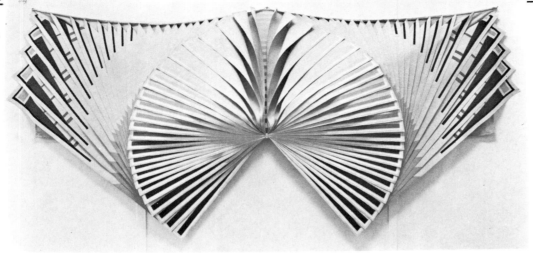

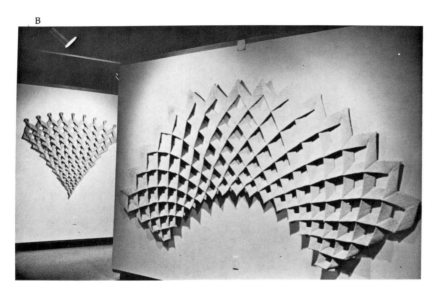

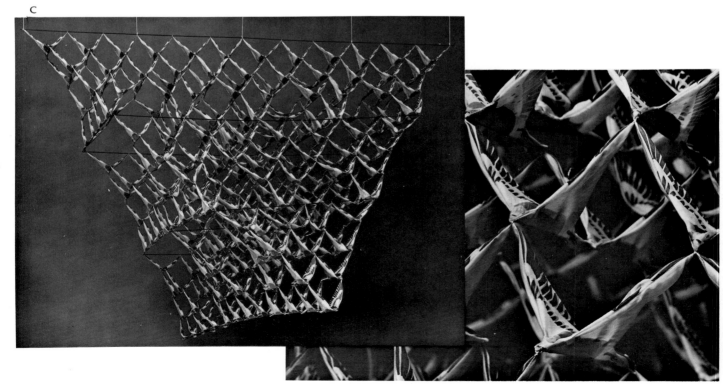

Pamela E. Becker
MEGA-COSM
Layered fabric construction; raw silk fabric, textile paint; 96 by 52 by 4 inches.

The word "mega-cosm" is Greek and means the universe or visible system of worlds.

B

Joan Michaels-Paque
LINES OF DEMARCATION
Knotted, woven, wrapped (J.M.P. penetrating planes technique); polished cotton; 12 feet, 2 inches by 5 feet, 6 inches by 2 inches.

My work/philosophy reflects my interests in topology and constructivism and my attempts to use them in unique, unorthodox ways.

C

Leena Marjatia Jokinen
THE FLIGHT OR THE NIGHTMARE OF A PILOT
Silk-screened; silk, fiber reactive pigment; 59 by 71 inches.

A

Katherine Tilton McMahon
SHIVER
Woven tapestry, slightly stuffed; wool, linen, rayon, silk, metallics; 38 by 42 by 3 inches.

This tapestry is part of a series of shaped, three-dimensional tapestries. In this series, I was working at stretching the limits of the loom and revising the limits of tapestry weave.

B

Arturo Alonzo Sandoval
DRAPED FILM GRID
Woven collage; bleached 16mm color movie film, opalescent mylar, acrylic polymer medium eyelets; 115 by 95 by 12 inches.

My inspiration was the transparency of insect wings which gave me the idea for the shaping and colors finally achieved.

C

Judith Rosenberg
UNINHABITED ISLAND
Woven, using wire armature as the loom; cotton, linen, wool, wire armature; 36 by 32 by 18 inches.

A

B

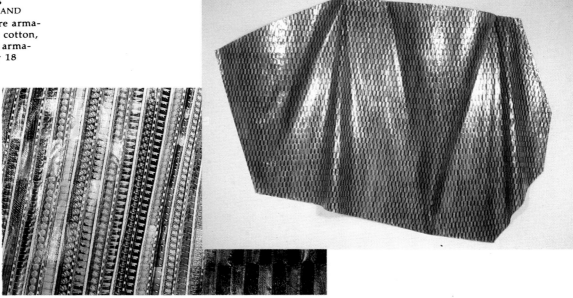

C

A

A
Jacqueline L. Fogel
ASCENDENCE
Boumaki, gouache;
Japanese paper, metallic
thread, silk, plexiglass; 24
by 29 by 8 inches.

B
Elizabeth Griffin
THE TIME BEFORE
THE TIME AFTER
Double woven, furled,
warp manipulation tech-
niques; wool, cotton,
linen; 60 by 48 by 3
inches.

B

A
Naomi Kane
DELTA CHOSE II
Woven; handspun wool,
defracted mylar; 54 by 65
inches.

B
Janice Lessman-Moss
GOING GREEN
Industrial felt, aluminum
rods, pearl cotton; 44 by
26 inches.

A

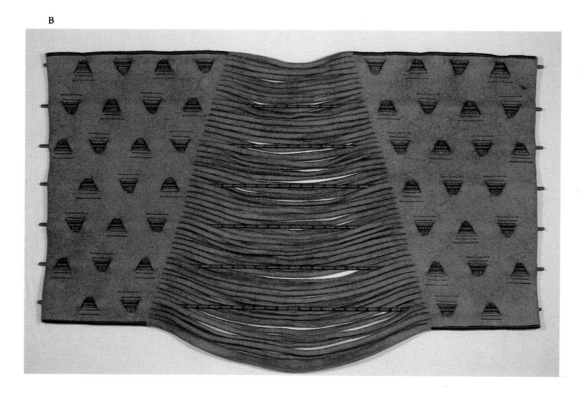

B

A

B

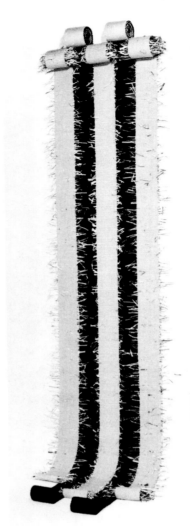

C

A
Tina Takayanagi Barnet
1 AM
Woven; linen, wire, wood; 27½ by 31½ by 11 inches. Photo by Tim Thayer.

This sculpture consists of handwoven linen panels which are supported by wooden dowels. Wire in the supplementary warp enables the flaps to maintain an open position.

B
Bonnie Rubenstein
MODEL SUITES
Woven; cotton, newspaper; 20 by 66 by 14 inches.

C
Dolly Curtis
DOUBLE RAINBOW
Woven environmental sculpture, ribbons woven in warp face weave; cotton thread, 14 ribbons, 8 inches by 21 feet each.

This woven environmental sculpture was installed in the theatre lobby of the Paul Mellon Arts Center at the Choate School in Wallingford, Connecticut.

A

Margo Shermeta
COPPER WHEAT
Woven (supplementary warp), dyed; cotton, rayon, silk; 44 by 75 by 4 inches.

B

Priscilla Sage
AZURE SYMPHYSIS
Machine and hand stitched; disperse dyes heat transfered to mylar polyester silver fabric which covers polyurethane; 24 by 63 by 24 inches. Photo by Kathleen Saccopoulos.

C

Mary Kester
THREE RESIST
Woven tapestry, multiple layer; wool, cotton, linen; 76 by 47 by 2 inches.

D

Anatoly Chernishov
UNTITLED
Woven tapestry; polyester, polypropylene; 75 by 80 by 2 inches.

This tapestry is one of the series of so-called "changeable" tapestries. Elements of this tapestry can be altered to create another composition. This idea was developed by Agam in sculpture but in my tapestries, even the elements themselves could change their form due to the pliability of the material.

A

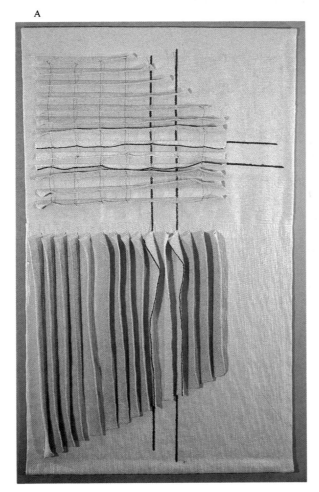

B

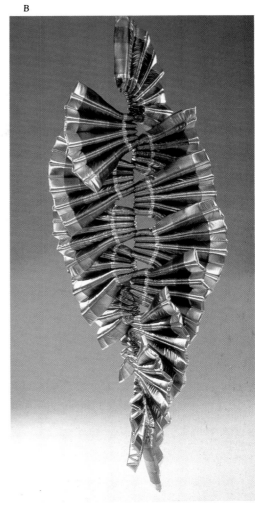

C

D

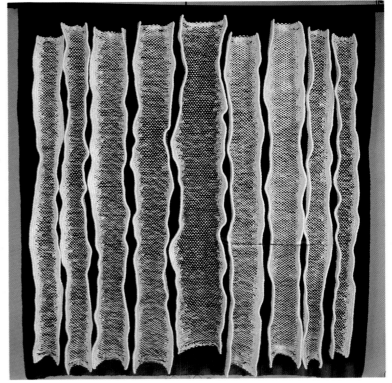

A

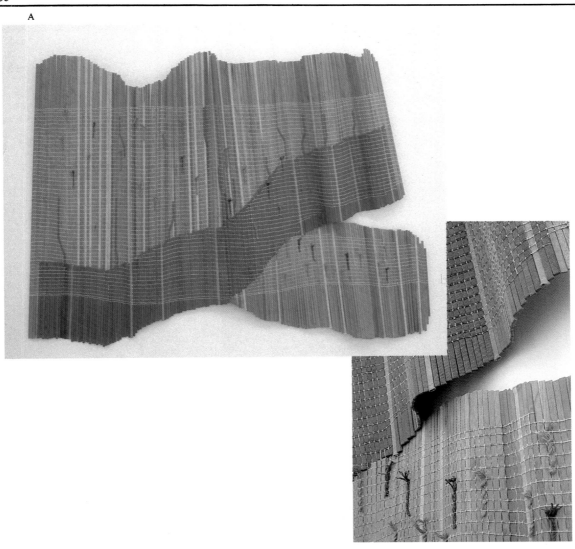

A
Jorie Johnson
CALIFORNIA SERIES III,
WIND FENCE
Woven, laced; mahogany
and redwood slatting,
linen, cotton, brass
webbing; 77 by 56 by 9
inches. Photo by Jon
Grass.

*I have always pulled away
from singular planed or tradi-
tionally square or rectangular
artwork. Therefore, the tightly
woven finished fabric is laced
onto a frame of irregular
curvature; creating an interesting, undulating movement
away from and into the plane
of the existing wall.*

B
Susan Warner Keene
METAPHORIC LANDSCAPE:
CALLANISH
Flax, cotton, dye, acrylic
medium; 138 by 72 by 3
inches. Photo by Peter
Newman.

B

Jean Hewes
PILLARS
Appliqued; silk, rayon,
brocade, cotton, poly-
ester; 92 by 95 inches.

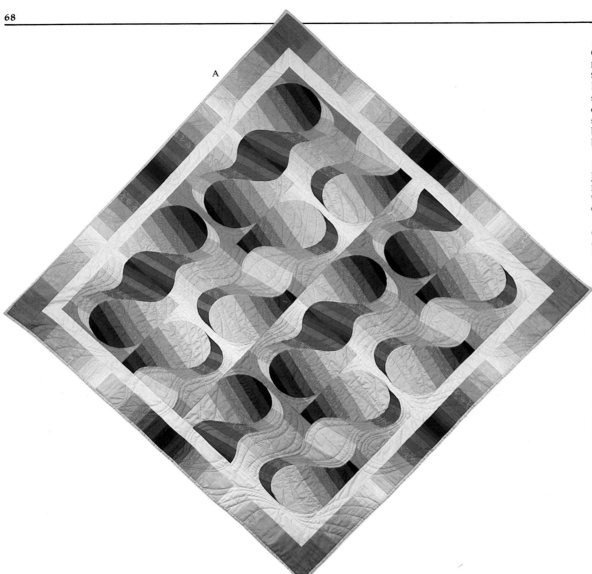

A

B

C

A
Gerlinde Anderson
FLAMINGOS ALONG THE
SHORE
Machine pieced (curved
slam construction), hand
quilted; cotton, cotton
sateen, chintz, polyester
batting, cotton thread; 60
by 60 inches.

B
Judi Warren
INTERIOR/EXTERIOR
WINDOWSCAPE:
OCTOBER MORNING
Machine pieced, appli-
qued, hand quilted;
cotton, viscose satin; 47
by 49 inches.

*Combining the applique
process with pieced areas
enables me to explore the
pictorial images I have done
before as paintings and to see
those images translated into the
textural surface achieved
through the quilting. The
quilted line becomes very much
like a drawn line.*

C
Charlene Burningham
COLOR MODULATION
Quilted; cotton, blends; 6
by 6 feet.

A
Sheila Meyer
REFLECTIONS II
Machine pieced, hand
quilted; cotton fabric,
polyester batting; 54 by
54 inches.

B
Mary G. Reida
ZIGGURAT
Hand quilted, machine
pieced; cotton; 77 by 73
inches.

*I wanted to achieve multi-
dimensional planes and shapes
which transcend the simple
rectangular log cabin block.*

C
Donna J. Katz
DRAGON FLY PAPER
Hand painted, pieced,
quilted; cotton muslin,
cotton/polyester, poly-
ester batting; 6 by 6 feet.

A

B

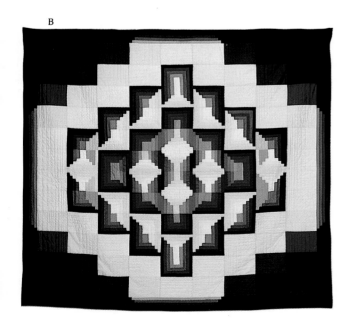

C

A

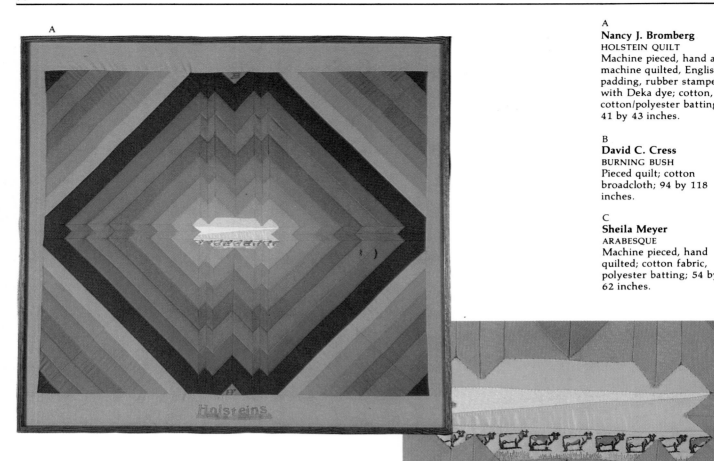

B

C

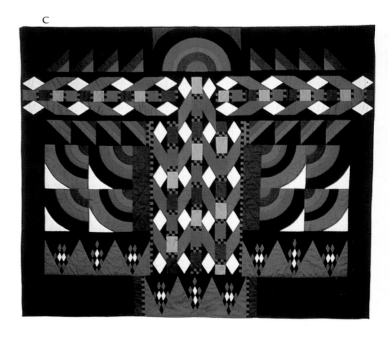

A
Nancy J. Bromberg
HOLSTEIN QUILT
Machine pieced, hand and
machine quilted, English
padding, rubber stamped
with Deka dye; cotton,
cotton/polyester batting;
41 by 43 inches.

B
David C. Cress
BURNING BUSH
Pieced quilt; cotton
broadcloth; 94 by 118
inches.

C
Sheila Meyer
ARABESQUE
Machine pieced, hand
quilted; cotton fabric,
polyester batting; 54 by
62 inches.

A
Margot Strand Jensen
IT CROSSED MY MIND
Hand appliqued, machine
pieced, machine quilted;
cotton, blends; 46 by 45
inches.

B
Esther Parkhurst
WATERFALL
Machine pieced, hand
quilted; cotton; 48 by 52
inches.

C
Gail A. Hanson
BE THE FIRST TO GET
YOUR MARBLES HOME
Quilted; commercially
dyed cotton and cotton/
polyester; 77 by 44
inches.

B
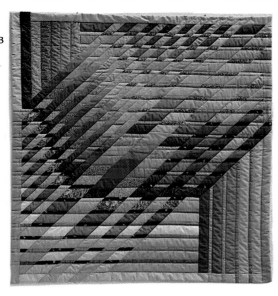

A
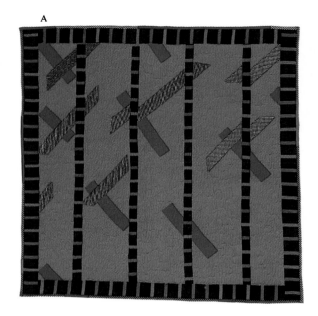

C
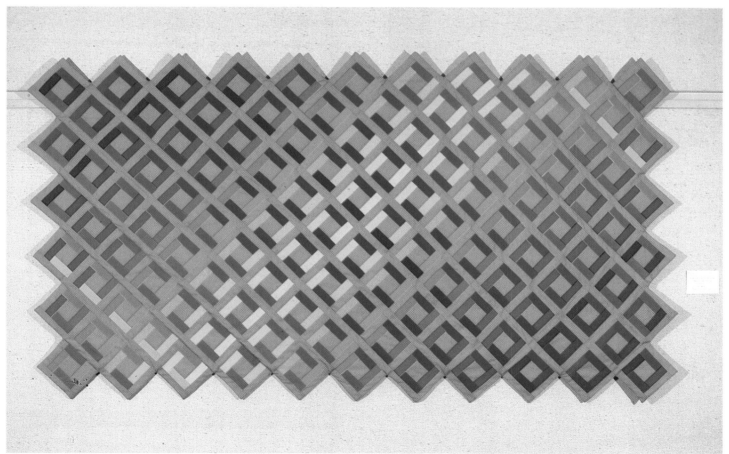

A

A
Jean V. Johnson
LIGHT IN THE FOREST
Machine pieced (Seminole tradition), hand quilted, mounted on stretcher; cotton, blends, silk for the stream; 24 by 44 inches.

B
Lucretia L. Romey
RED SHEDS
Hand quilted; cotton, cotton blends, fiberfill; 40 by 52 inches.

I am primarily a watercolor painter by profession who sews images into fabric pictures. Generally, I cut inch wide strips of fabric and I arrange about 35 different colors of the fabric strips on a rack. I work "free hand" as a painter would and the rack of colors is my palette.

B

A

Carolyn Muller
DEAR HERTHA,
—WISH YOU WERE HERE
Appliqued, quilted,
piecework; cotton, velvet,
organdy, moire,
corduroy; 40 by 48
inches. Photo by Don
Muller.

*This quilt was done in
memory of my mother and is a
very personal piece. It is also a
continuation of the concept I
strive to portray in all of my
quilts: the concept of space. In
this instance, it is space in
time - past versus present.
Quilted by Wiletta Farris.*

B

Carolyn Muller
WINTER'S END
Appliqued, quilted, strip
pieced, piecework; velvet,
corduroy, moire,
organdy, cotton, wool; 60
by 63 inches. Photo by
Don Muller.

*WINTER'S END was inspired
after studying the fields as the
winter season terminated. The
landscape appeared to
anticipate the coming of the
next season - a new time. I
was motivated to convey this
concept of transition in time.
Quilted by Wiletta Farris.*

A

B

A

A
Ann Bird
RUNNER
Machine appliqued,
machine quilted; cotton
blends, cotton, satin; 10
by 3 feet.

B
Judy Wasserman Hearst
DREAM OF THE '80S
Hand appliqued, hand
quilted; cotton, polyester
batting; 42 by 57 inches.

*This quilt was a piece that I
collaborated on with Edward
Larson, a quilt designer known
for his folk art style. I came
up with the subject matter, he
did the design and I made the
quilt.*

C
Rebekka Seigel
PAPER DOLL QUILT
Batiked and pieced back-
ground, appliqued and
reverse appliqued
costumes; cotton, poly-
ester/cotton blend, beads,
polyester batting; 66 by
66 inches.

*The inspiration for this quilt
came from the paper dolls I
played with in the '50s. The
dresses in themselves are little
quilts that are attached to the
larger piece with Velcro so
they can be removed and placed
on the doll (also attached with
Velcro).*

A

Ann Bird
NEON SERIES: INNER
DANCER
Reverse appliqued,
machine quilted; cotton;
50 by 40 inches.

*I am interested in the variety
of images and statements that
can be made artistically with
the medium of fabric and the
tools of needle and thread. In
this case, my love of dance is
expressed in a graphic way.*

B

M. A. Klein
THE COCKTAIL PARTY
Appliqued, stitched, hand
quilted; cotton/polyester,
linen; 34 by 52 inches.

C

Connie M. Lehman
BLACK FOREST COYOTE
Machine quilted, wax
resist; cotton, Versatex
dye; 43 by 42 inches.

A

B

C

A
Allyson Turner
AMEBADON
Hand quilted, hand pieced; cotton/polyester fabric and batting; 71 by 86 inches. Photo by Henry Vanderdraay.

B
Adele Quimby
BRANCH OF THE FAITH
Appliqued, pieced, hand quilted; cotton fabric; 58 by 78 inches.

Feeling an interrelationship between floor, wall and bed covering through the ages, I attempted to adapt some of the traditional geometric patterns, beauty, symmetry and harmony of Caucasian rugs to an appliqued quilt.

C
Heidi Darr-Hope
EXPECTING
Quilted; cyanotype and kallitype on cotton muslin and satin, surface embellished with Procion dye, colored pencils, ribbons, silk thread, metallic thread, buttons, sequins, glass beads; 39 by 44 inches.

There is much energy and information held within the traditional quilt form. The scraps of cloth saved and collected are fragments of the creator's existence. These works, from the "Patterned Narrative Series", utilize the quilt form as a means of communicating autobiographical experiences, observations and perceptions.

A
Nancy N. Erickson
JUPITER WATCH OVER
CAPYBARALAND
Painted, machine
stitched; Versatex paint,
cotton, satin; 98 by 92
inches. Photo by Nancy
N. Erickson.

*Capybara are four feet, 160
pound rodents (the world's
largest) who live in the river
banks of Uruguay and other
South American countries.
They are friendly, placid,
communal, vegetarian and
make peculiar noises. Accord-
ing to the Scientific Director of
the World Wildlife Fund,
Capybara are used as seeing-
eye animals; they can be tamed
and trained like dogs.*

B
Nancy N. Erickson
THE LAST DANCE OF FALL
Machine stitched; cotton,
velvet, satin; 9½ by 9
feet. Photo by Jon
Schulman.

A

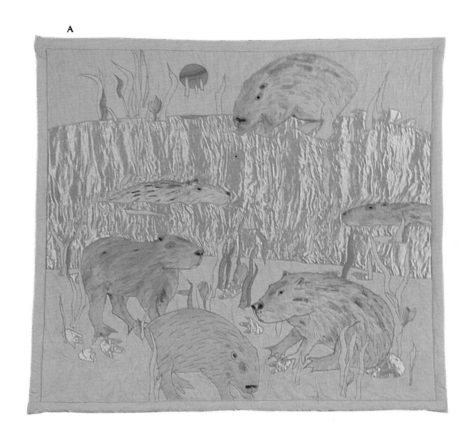

B

78

A

B

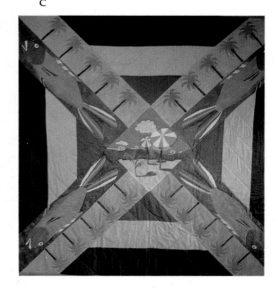

C

A
Anne Comfort Morrell
SEASONS OF MY LIFE
Machine appliqued, hand
embroidered and quilted;
cotton; 100 by 112
inches.

*This quilt is a farm and
family portrait surrounded by
twenty-two self-portraits
arranged seasonally to show
my work and pleasures on the
farm. It ties together old and
new quilt techniques as well as
"old fashioned" and modern
lifestyles.*

B
Faye G. Anderson
BYE BYE DUBROVNIK
Pieced, appliqued,
embroidered, quilted;
cotton, acetate; 63 by 43
inches.
*This is a fiber postcard of a
trip to Yugoslavia.*

C
Donna J. Katz
BEACH BLANKET
Hand painted, pieced,
quilted; cotton muslin,
cotton/polyester, poly-
ester batting; 6 by 6 feet.

*I like to use juxtaposition,
diverse combinations of
elements. I call this a painted
quilt or a quilted painting. In
my work, I think I visualize
fantasy. I take silliness
seriously and vice versa.*

A

**Marilyn Lawrance
Harrison**
TEN TURNIPS
Quilted, batiked, wax
resist; Procion dye,
viscose satin, Dacron
batting; 40 by 60 inches.

*August in south Florida is not
the best season to work on
heavy quilting, yet this "veggie
patch" has done better than
any garden I ever planted.*

B

Rebekka Seigel
DUCK POND
Batiked, reverse ap-
pliqued, appliqued,
pieced, embroidered,
direct dyed; cotton,
rayon, polyester batting;
90 by 120 inches.

A

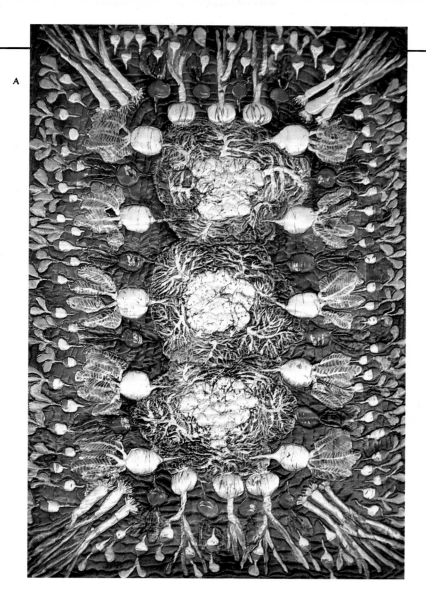

B

A

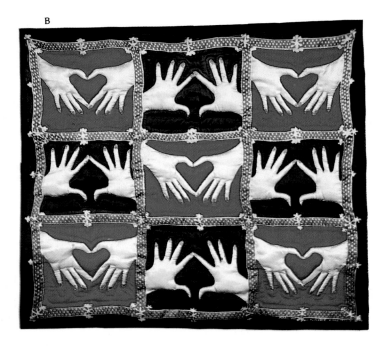

B

C

A
Solveig Ronnqvist
MAYA
Machine pieced, hand quilted, trapunto center, patchwork outer area; polished cotton/polyester, cotton; 31 by 31 inches.

B
Marilyn Lawrance Harrison
HEARTS AND SPADES
Batiked, hand and machine quilted, wax resist; viscose rayon, Dacron fill and batting, Procion dye; 41 by 37 inches.

I love to observe children seeing this piece for the first time. They always see the hearts and spades immediately and then gleefully show them to their parents who sometimes have a hard time getting past the hands.

C
Patsy Allen
DECO SERIES #1
Machine pieced, appliqued, quilted; cotton, cotton blend fabric, polyester batting; 23 by 3½ feet. Photo by A. Doren.

My designs deal primarily with spatial relationships - the break up of space and the movement of shapes, lines and colors through that space. This work was physically demanding because the composition, continuous across four panels with 6 inch spaces, had to match perfectly when installed. I constructed the quilt top almost entirely in one piece then cut it into four sections, taking out the 6 inch squares.

A
Nancy Herman
TWO MOROCCAN
MEASURES
Pieced, appliqued; silk,
satin, cotton; 6 by 6 feet.

A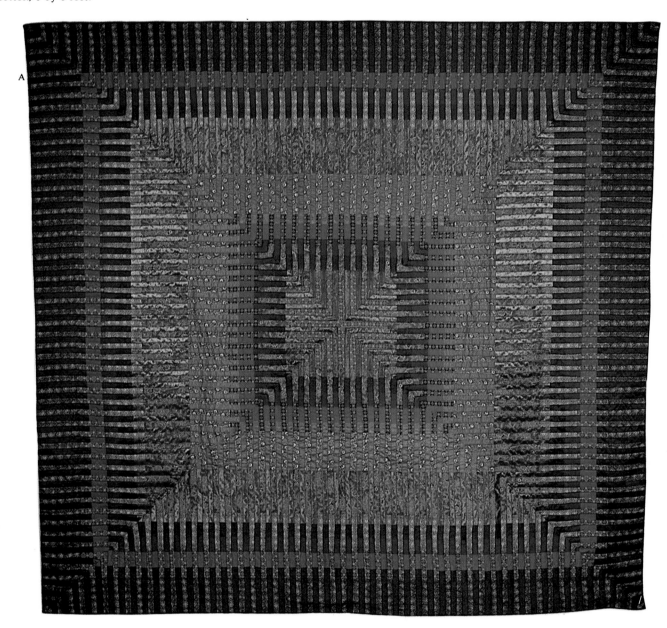

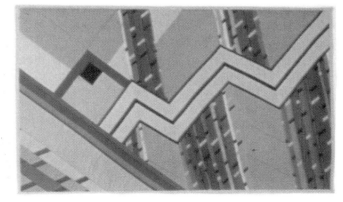

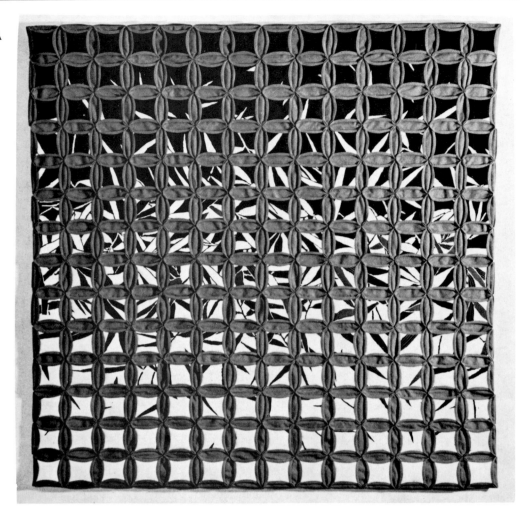

A

B

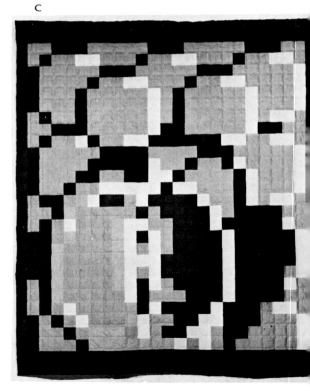

C

A
Margaret Stephenson Coole
WINDOW SHADES - BLACK AND WHITE I
Folded fabric, reassembled print applique; hand dyed cotton, cotton print; 36 by 36 inches.

B
Nancy Gipple
THINKING ABOUT HER ROLLER COASTER RIDE, HOPING SHE CAN GET HERSELF OFF
Machine quilted; mixed cotton; 94 by 74 inches. Photo by John Tressman.

C
Nannette Cotton
ORANGES
Hand quilted; cotton; 52 by 63 inches.

In Sanskrit, the verb for "to be" also means "to grow". We must continue to grow within ourselves in order to be really alive. Plants and other growing things inspire me and I enjoy capturing their living colors.

A
Patricia Malarcher
HOMAGE TO KARL
VON FRISCH
Hand and machine
stitched, appliqued;
metallized mylar, cotton
and rayon thread, linen,
canvas; 56 by 50 inches.
Photo by Kay Ritta.

B
Esther Parkhurst
JOSEPH'S COAT
Machine pieced, hand
quilted; cotton; 70 by 55
inches.

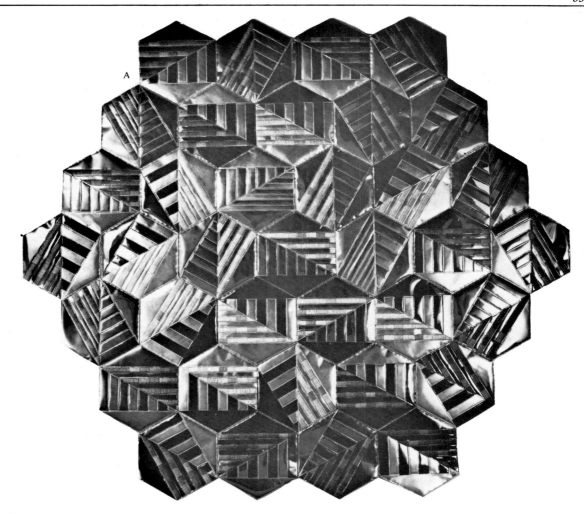

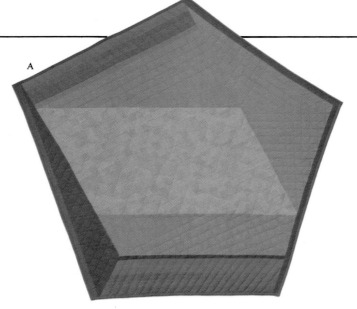

A

B

C

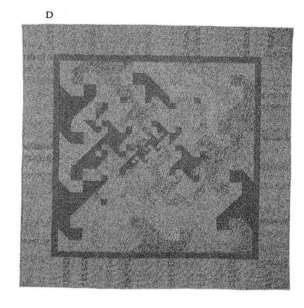

D

A
Debra Millard
PENTA-SQUARES
Machine pieced, hand quilted; hand dyed cotton fabric, Procion fiber reactive dye; 40 by 40 inches.

B
Susan Denton
COSMIC CASTLE
Hand and machine pieced, hand appliqued, quilted; cotton, silk, rayon, polyester batting; 60 by 60 inches.

C
Patricia White
TSUNAMI
Machine pieced, hand quilted; cotton top and lining, cotton batting; 84 by 96 inches.

D
Pamela Gustavson Johnson
MONKEY WRENCH II
Machine pieced, hand quilted; cotton, polyester batting; 66½ by 66½ inches.

A

Gail A. Hanson
NINETY-EIGHT POINT SIX
IN THE SHADE AND RISING
Quilted; commercially
dyed cotton and cotton/
polyester; 67 by 59
inches.

B

Lynne Sward
BLACK AND WHITE AND
TECHNICOLOR - TWO
Hand pieced, appliqued,
padded; cotton/polyester;
34½ by 19½ inches.

*My love affair with motion
pictures started at a very early
age and this love affair
inspired the design for BLACK
AND WHITE AND
TECHNICOLOR - ONE
which led to the present series
employing color, black and
white and motion.*

A

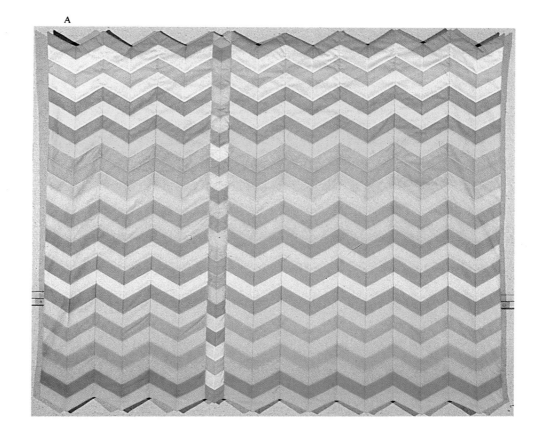

B

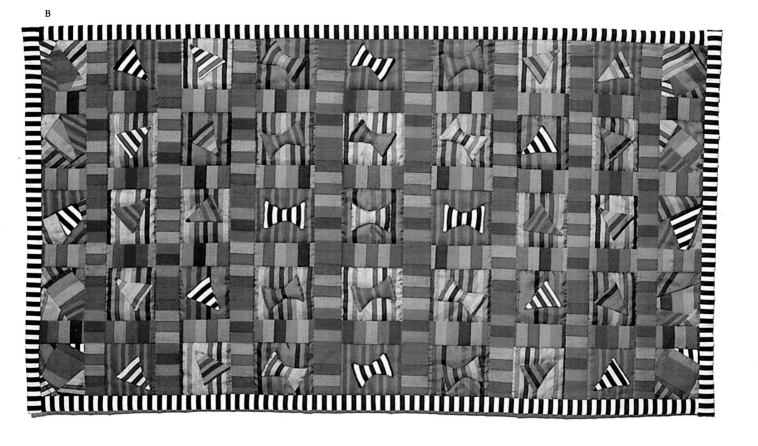

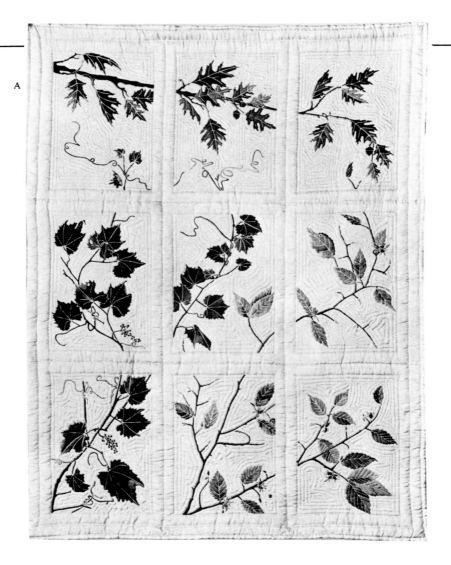

A

A
H. Jeannette Shanks
THROUGH MY WINDOW
Hand painted, hand
quilted; silk; 54 by 72
inches.

B
Lenda B. DuBose
QUILTED QUADRAPARTITE
ICON
Machine pieced, hand
quilted with copper plate
etchings printed on
muslin; 35 by 35 inches.
Photo by Chris Mounger.

*The plates were made by my
printmaker husband for a
series of etchings based (somewhat loosely) on the four
evangelists from the "Book of
Kells". The discovery that
etchings can be printed quite
accurately on cloth has opened
new possibilities for me
including visual imagery in
fiber pieces and collaboration
between artists in two media.*

A
Katy Gilmore
WARM BOOTS
Screen printed, machine
pieced, hand quilted;
cotton muslin, polyester
batting; 68 by 76 inches.

B
Susan M. Sharpe
KITCHEN MUSIC
Machine quilted, direct
dyed; cotton sailcloth,
fiber reactive dye; 56 by
60 inches. Photo by
Frank Stroh.

A

B

A

B

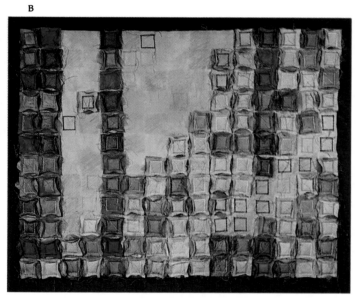

C

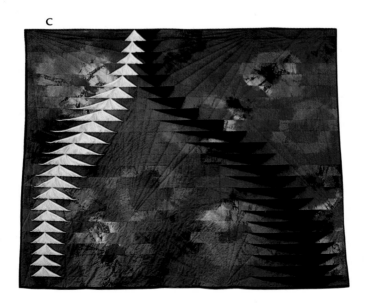

A
Nancy E. Rial
GRID
Hand quilted; cotton velveteen, bonded polyester fiberfill, cotton back; 9 by 9 feet.

The hand quilting was done by Carol Marracello and Nancy Rial and the quilt has been in progress for two years. Within the rigid geometric framework with which I like to work, I wanted to create a quality of light (penetrating, emerging). The "light" is accomplished by changing colors of the cotton velveteen strips that separate the squares on the grid.

B
Judith West
HAUNTED MOSAIC
Quilted, appliqued, drawn; cotton fabric, nylon net, sewing thread, ink, dye, color pencils; 30 by 24 inches.

HAUNTED MOSAIC deals with the varying degrees of physical and spiritual being. Drawn squares suggest the ephemeral while appliqued squares, stitching and stuffed pillows represent greater degrees of substantial being.

C
Chris and Jacquelyn Faulkner
DREAMING OF THE PHAROAHS
Pieced, quilted; tie-dyed cotton (by Jennifer Brooke), velvet; 68 by 59 inches.

In each dimension of this piece, the design element was manipulated to create a dream image: regular shapes formed in the process of tie-dyeing were disjointed by strip piecing, "pyramids" trail through the ether, and horizons tilt and overlap.

A
Janice Anthony
GREAT WALL OF CHINA
Machine and hand pieced,
hand quilted; cotton
fabrics, polyester batting;
82 by 85 inches.

*The Great Wall fascinated me
because of its contradictory
qualities: stone fortresses with
a delicacy of line across the
landscape like Christo's
"Running Fence". The Wall
has a life of its own, ageless
and it is the only man-made
object visible from space.*

B
**Marilyn McKenzie
Chaffee**
DEL RIO QUILT
Pieced, hand quilted;
cotton, polyester batting;
50 by 50 inches.

A

B

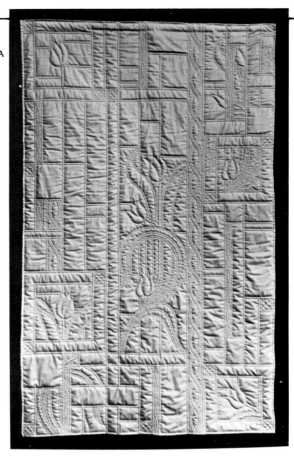

A

Sue H. Rodgers
VICTORIAN WINDOWS
Hand quilted, trapunto;
cotton/polyester polished
cotton, polyester batting,
acrylic yarn; 36 by 59
inches.

B

Mary Frances Ellison
UNTITLED
Hand quilted; cotton
chintz back, cotton
batting, cotton/polyester
face; 94 by 104 inches.

*This piece was inspired by a
collaboration with a wood-
worker friend who designed a
handmade walnut bed and
needed a coverlet for his piece.*

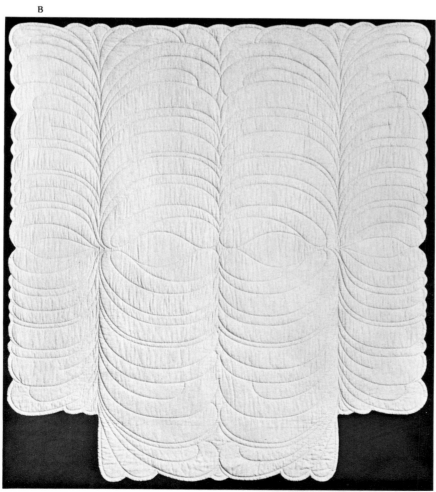

B

A
Christina Buck
SUNLIT PATHS
Machine pieced, hand
quilted; cotton, cotton
blend fabric, polyester
batting; 42 by 36 inches.
Photo by Christina Buck.

*In this series, I have been
working directly with the
fabric without drawing
preliminary sketches. I aim for
a complicated surface with an
illusion of depth and the
appearance of many folds and
different surfaces weaving over
and behind each other.*

B
Sylvia Kern
PAYING HOMAGE TO
JEAN RAY LAURY
Quilted; felt, teletype
paper, fiberfill; 25 by 25
inches. Photo by Jon
Cizak.

*My background in textiles and
quilting led me to explore the
possibilities of using traditional quilt patterns with non-
traditional fibers.*

C
Linda MacDonald
RUTH FRESNO'S DREAM
Machine pieced, hand
appliqued and quilted;
cotton, polyester batting;
82 by 82 inches. Photo by
Jim Cochran.

*I choose the American quilt as
the presentation-medium for
my illusionistic images. The
largeness of the image window
coupled with the tactile fabric
composition and the tradition
of something truly American
done by American women
compels me to joyfully embrace
this art form.*

A

B

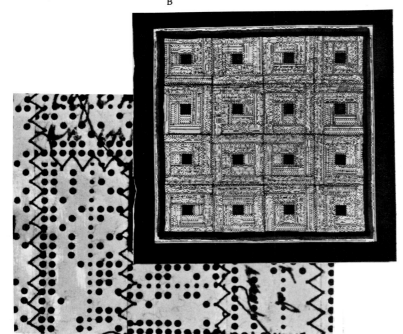

C

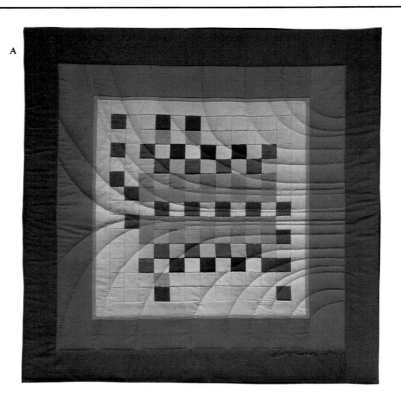

A

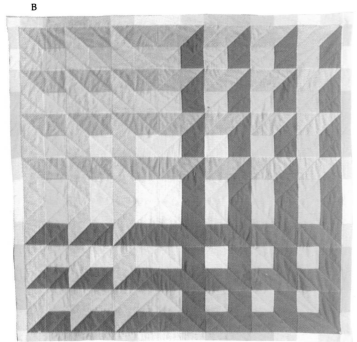

B

C

A
Betty Amador
JOSE CHOICE
Hand quilted, cotton patchwork; 28 by 29 inches.

B
Nancy Rowe
ATTIC WINDOWS-SUNSET
Machine pieced and quilted; cotton fabric, cotton/polyester batting, nylon thread; 44 by 44 inches.

C
Alice Newton
SPRING RAINS
Machine pieced, hand quilted; cotton fabric, polyester batting; 28 by 28 inches.

This is the third of a four part series, "Blue Ridge Sunrise". Every window in my home affords a panoramic view of the Blue Ridge Mountains of West Virginia, Virginia and Maryland, and for several years I have been listening to the local people talk about the changes in colors in the mountains that come with the subtle changes in the weather. SPRING RAIN *focuses on the hill in bloom with redbud, peach, apple and dogwood trees appearing through the gentle rain and an early morning rainbow.*

Jayn Thomas
LIVE WIRE
Woven, ikat dyed; mer-
cerized cotton and silk
sewing thread; 57 by 144
inches. Photo by David
Caras.

A

B

C

D

A
Elizabeth Abeel
QUIET MOMENTS
Traditional dipped batik, direct application of dye; pima cotton, fiber reactive dye; 26 by 40 inches.

B
T. A. Culshaw
COWBOY IN BLUE, **#1**
Batiked using traditional method dyebath; Procion dye, wax resist, cotton; 24 by 32 inches.

C
Linda Rugel
GUIDING TOUCH
Batiked; cotton muslin, aniline dye; 26½ by 33¾ inches (framed).

D
Karen Fields Moss
ANIMAL FAIR
Direct dye on silk, tjanted wax resist, hand painted; silk satin, Procion dye; 48 by 54 inches.

A

Leong Chan
FACELESS HEROES, I
Screen printed, machine
sewn; unwashed, un-
bleached calico, cotton
thread; 35 by 61 inches.

B

Connie Ellis
TONY
Batiked, direct dyed;
China silk, Procion and
Naphthol dyes, wax
resist; 36 by 52 inches.

C

Fern Helfand
REPETITIONS SERIES,
STONE FIGURE
Van Dyke brown print
on cotton, hand colored
with Prisma colors and
oil pastels, trapunto; 8 by
5 feet.

*This series explores in form
and content the repeated atti-
tudes and reactions which
sometimes occur within sexual
relationships.*

D

Fern Helfand
REPETITIONS SERIES,
WALKING WOMAN
Trapunto relief sculpture,
hand colored with oil
pastels and pencil
crayons, Van Dyke
brown print on cotton;
10 by 4 feet.

A

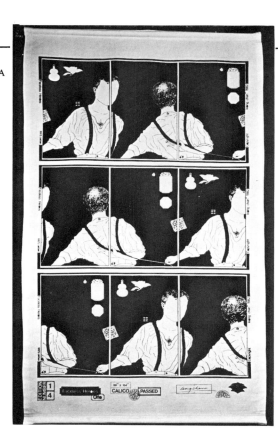

B

C

D

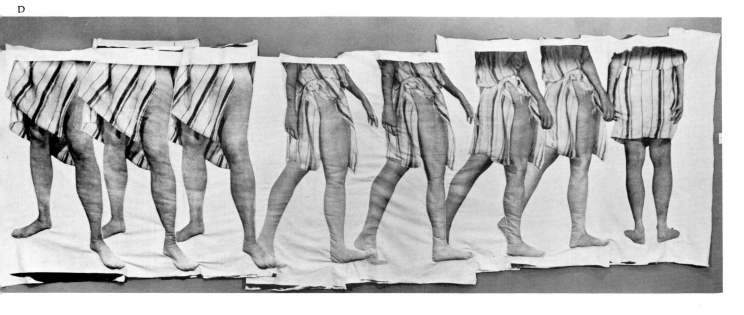

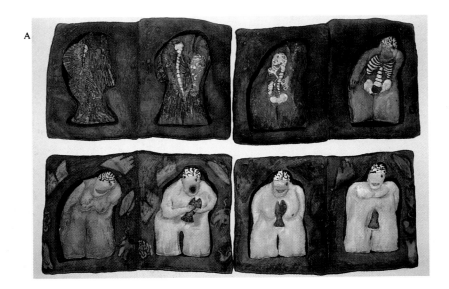

A

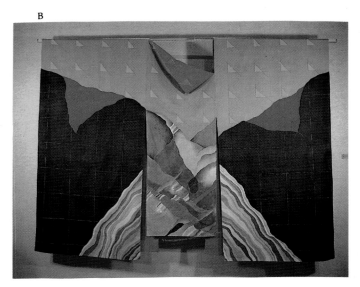

B

C

D

A
Barbara F. Lambert
METAMORPHOSIS OR THE
ORIGINATION OF THE
COD PIECE
Batiked, direct dyed;
Procion dye, cotton,
stuffed with polyester
fiberfill; 60 by 42 by 3
inches.

B
Patricia L. Brown
JOSEPHE'S HAUTE COUTURE
Hand painted, silk-
screened, hand stitched;
cotton, embroidery floss;
75 by 85 inches.

C
Barbara Klaer
LULLABY FOR JAKE
Painted, batiked; cotton
muslin, fiber reactive
dye; 30 by 20 inches.
Photo by Jon Pais.

*Working in a combination of
traditional batik techniques
and direct painting of dyes, I
try to utilize the fluidity of the
materials to express the
mystery of dream stories and
inner reflections.*

D
Barbara Klaer
TEN YEAR COFFEE BREAK
Painted, batiked; cotton,
fiber reactive dye; 30 by
41 inches. Photo by Jon
Pais.

A
Dona Dowling Abt
HOMAGE TO VANITY
Photo silk-screened, film
positive; rayon and gold
thread applied to hand
dyed canvas mounted on
painted wood; 22 by 14
inches.

B
Ellen Gunn
PRIMAVERA
Batiked; silk, aniline dye;
30 by 36 inches.

C
Beth Holyoke
DINOSAUR WINDOW
Batiked, stitched, drawn,
machine quilted; cotton,
linen, fiber reactive dye,
ink, polyester fiberfill; 39
by 24 inches.

A

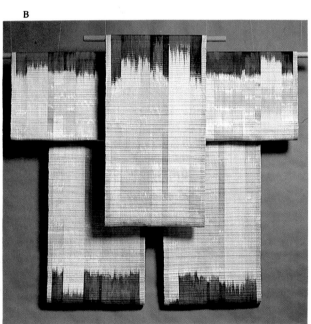

B

C

A
Patricia L. Brown
LAND TO WATER
Hand painted, hand stitched; cotton, embroidery floss, 105 by 65 inches.

B
Morgan Elizabeth Clifford
FREE-FALL
Woven, warp faced cotton ikat; 60 by 72 by 10 inches.

I work in ikat because of the spontaneity and energy inherent in the technique. It's a very intuitive form of creativity requiring lots of risks which keep the process and final work very alive and exciting for me.

C
Carol Van Heerden
RITUAL GARMENT
Woven, silk-screened warp, ikat, dip dyed; linen, Procion dye; 57 by 20 inches. Photo by Ken Clark.

A
Teresa Nomura
ASCENDING TRIANGLES
Dyed, sprayed, hand
painted; linen, cotton; 55
by 72 inches.

B
Lesley Richmond
UNTITLED
Wax resist, painted with
liquid Procion dyes; silk
shantung; 45 inches
wide.

C
Mary C. Birckhead
WATER MOODS
Woven (double ikat tech-
nique); cotton, Procion
dye; 35 by 45 inches.

A

B

C

A

B

C

A
H. Jeannette Shanks
IN FLIGHT
Hand painted; silk, floating banners suspended at 20-degree angle on mono-filament within plexiglass mount; 27 by 96 inches.

B
Gary Fey
FIESTA ISLE #3
Hand painted; silk crepe de Chine, fiber reactive dye; 16 by 20 inches.

The landscapes seen here were inspired from my original pastel drawings done on location. In my outdoor studio, I transfer the drawings to the silk fiber by first outlining the entire scene in wax. Fiber reactive dyes are applied by hand. When the painting process is completed the piece is dry cleaned and displayed similar to stained glass in windows, etc., allowing light to interact with the dyed fibers.

C
Mary Tyler
SHINE I
Woven, warp faced weave in a loom controlled card weaving pattern, hand dyed silk ikat with supplementary warps added and removed; 22 by 21 inches.

My work is an exploration of color and the illusion of depth and motion created by the interaction of colors. This piece is three separate panels hung as one.

A
Celia Carl Anderson
A POINT OF CONTENTION
Batiked, padded,
stretched onto shaped
frame; velveteen, Procion
dye; 60 by 66 inches.

*I enjoy working with shaped
pieces and allowing the fiber to
become part of an architectural
space. This piece becomes part
of the corner but visually
brings the corner out to a flat
surface again.*

B
Joan Hausrath
CELEBRATION
Woven, warp faced, dip
dyed; wool with acrylic
slats at top and bottom;
44 by 40 inches.

*I design my wall hangings
with gradual color transitions
that either visually blend or
contrast with other colors.
Often producing spatial or
luminous effects, the colors are
contained within a horizontal
and vertical framework reflecting the woven structure of the
medium.*

C
Betty Vera
OVERTURE
Woven, ikat warp, hand
dyed weft inlay; noil silk,
chenille; 41 by 36 inches.
Photo by Veronica
Saddler.

A

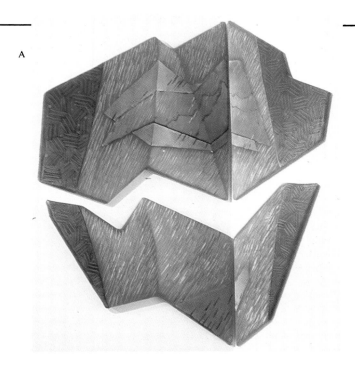

B

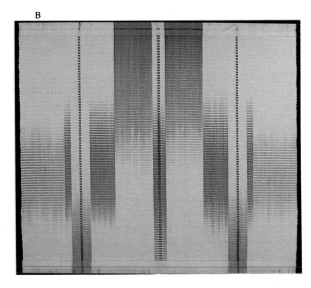

C

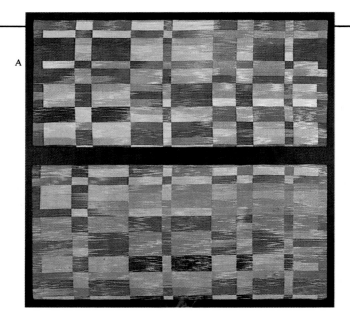

A

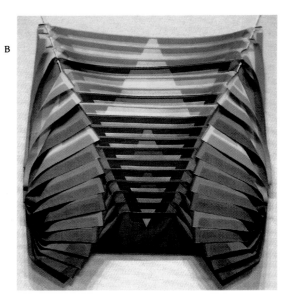

B

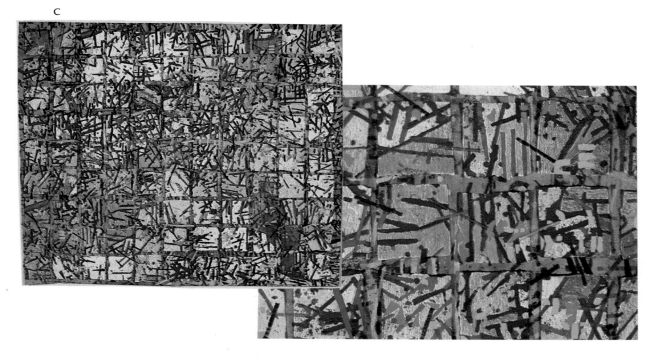

C

A
Dominie Nash
WESTERN FLIGHT
Eight-harness double
weave, ikat; cotton warp,
cotton, silk and rayon
weft; 36 by 32 inches.

B
Pamela E. Becker
RADIANT SYMMETRY
Layered, painted fabric
construction; cotton rope,
fabric with applied textile
paint; 36 by 42¼ by 5
inches.

RADIANT SYMMETRY *is
part of a series of constructed
forms recording one person's
reactions to and observations of
the rhythms and objects found
in the world.*

C
Lucy A. Jahns
PICKUP STICKS
Silk-screened on paper
and fabric, machine
embroidered, drawn;
fabric, thread, pencil,
paper, dye; 29 by 24
inches.

*In my work, I am most con-
cerned with color and pattern.
In this piece, I am also
involved in using paper and
fabric interchangeably in their
treatment.*

A

A

Jo Ann Giordano
TANKA II
Screen printed on fabric;
cotton, Versatex pig-
ment; 40 by 78 inches.

*I enjoy the magic of creating
spatial illusions and of experimenting with color and
pattern. My wall hangings
fulfill a spiritual need in my
life and contain personal
symbols that reflect my feelings
and ideas.*

B

PCTURCZYN
KARMA PEACOCK
Handpainted on silk;
aniline and acid dyes,
silver pigment, gutta; 36
by 88 inches.

*The banners in this series are
based on checkerboards. Each
banner makes an ostensibly
simple graphic statement.
Closer viewing reveals many
layers of movement, both in
the color and in the design
elements.*

C

Julie Kemble
NIRVANA
Hand painted, stretched
over plywood frames and
hinged; silk, French dyes,
backed with satin; 10 by
4 feet. Photo by Norman
Rittberg.

*For several years now, I've
been somewhat obsessed by the
idea of secret gardens. Having
already done several small
pieces on that theme I decided
the only way to work it out of
my system was to create
something I could sort of climb
into; my own small
environment.*

B

C

A

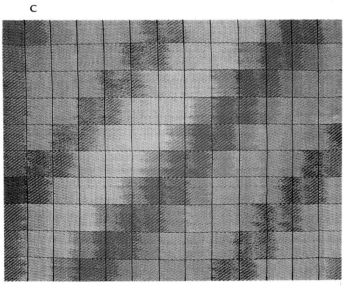

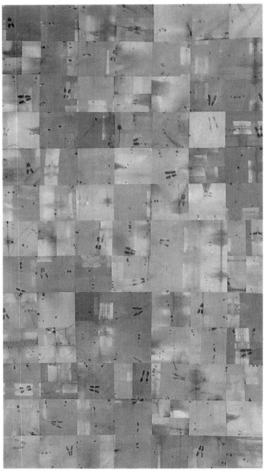

A
Barbara Lee Smith
THE MAGIC OF SAM LEE'S NAME
Machine embroidered; Inko dyed silk; 58 by 48 inches.

My work combines an informal, romantic, spontaneous approach when I apply the dyes and colors and a very formal, controlled structure when I superimpose the machine embroidery on the dyed silk.

B
Elizabeth Byrd
MITOSIS
Clamp resist dyed, pieced; cotton broadcloth, Procion dye; 31 by 54 inches.

C
J. Harrell
HOT LINES #5
Woven, rayon warp ikat, brocade, twill weave; Procion dye; 30 by 38 inches.

A
Diana Zoe Coop
PELICAN BAY AQUARIUM
Painted, sewn, embroid-
ered, stuffed; hand dyed
wool, Egyptian cotton,
Versatex dye, acrylic
paint; one of five panels.

*This was a commission piece
for a "hotel/boatel" on Gran-
ville Island in Vancouver,
B.C., Canada. My inspira-
tion was the underwater life
which abounds here on the
coast.*

B
Sharon Fay
FLAGSHIP
Silk-screened; cotton,
Procion dye; 4 by 6 feet.

C
Agnes Rev
SPRING MOSAIC
Wax resisted, painted;
silk, fiber reactive dye;
5½ by 18 inches.

A

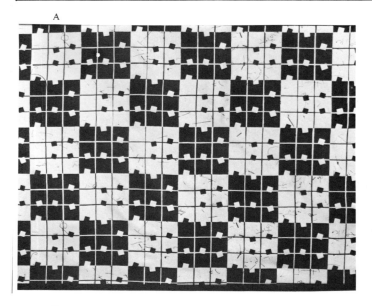

B

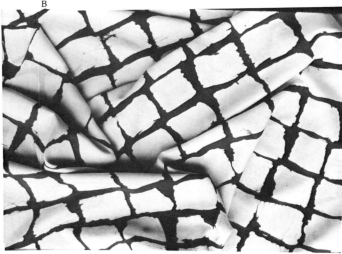

C

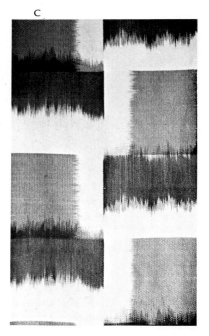

D

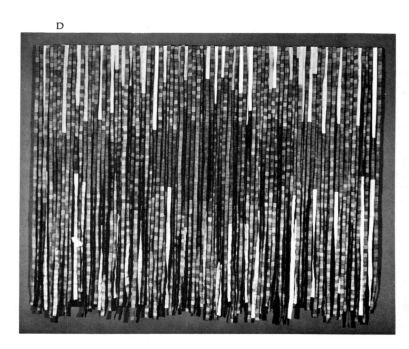

E

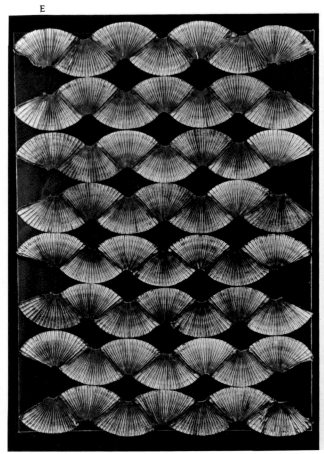

A
Zoe Woodruff Lancaster
HANKY PANKY
Screen-printed; water-based pigment on silk; 48 inches wide.

B
Kay Howell
UNTITLED
Batiked with scratch marks through wax; silk pongee, fiber reactive dye; 3 by 9 feet.

C
Lydia Van Gelder
COMPOUND IKAT FOR HIPPARI FABRIC
Woven; silk yarn, dyed cochineal weft, dyed madder warp.

D
Ann Williamson Hyman
MILKY WAY TIME WARP
Dyed, pieced; silk, cotton; 44 by 36 inches.

E
Tina Burris
RHYTHMS
Dyed using Japanese Nui-Shibori dyeing technique in the Mokume pattern; cotton muslin mounted on plexiglass; 15 by 21 inches. Photo by Ken Altshuler.

A
Tery Pellettier
WINDOW TOWARD
YOUNGSTOWN
Handpainted; French dye
on silk; 40 by 70 inches.

B
Amy Zerner
WITCHESSENCE
Mixed media collage,
tapestry and fabric; new
and antique fabrics and
trimmings, ribbon, lace,
color Xerox; 40½ by 37½
inches. Photo by
Rameshwar Das.

WITCHESSENCE *symbolizes*
Woman at the pinnacle of
personal power. Both the
animal energies and the mores
of her time are under her
watchful eye; balance and
harmony must be preserved.

C
Bonnie Lee Holland
BLUE JAZZY LADY
Hand painted; French
dye on China silk; 34 by
35 inches.

I enjoy using disparate design
elements and fusing them into
a unified whole. Jazz is
certainly an influence and
checkerboards are a current
theme.

D
Jeanne G. Costello
SPRING IS COMING
Painted; silk twill, French
aniline dye; 34 by 45
inches.

A

B

D

C

A

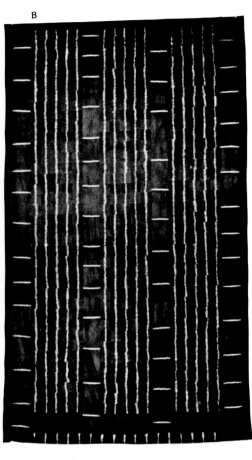

B

C

A

Darla Kalman
GRIDDLE CAKE I
Loom controlled double
weave interchange;
cotton, dip dyed warp;
16½ by 45¼ inches.

B

Beth Hay
NOMAD'S DOOR
Tie-dyed, batiked, pieced,
stitched; silk; 46 by 87
inches.

NOMAD'S DOOR *is a two-sided hanging.*

C

Ruth Parks
BAYOU
Woven (Sumba ikat tech-
nique); wool; 50 by 60
inches.

STITCHED, PRESSED, KNOTTED, ENTWINED

Renie Breskin Adams
BLANK PAGE,
MENTAL BUZZ
Stitched with knotting
and crocheting included
in the frame; pearl
cotton, cotton sewing
thread; 19 by 15¼ inches.

A

A

Jan Yatsko
RETURN OF HALEY'S COMET
Coiled wool with insert
of plastic cylinder filled
with coiled discs and
ribbon; 16 by 15 by 5½
inches. Photo by Scott
Kriner.

B

Flo Hoppe
SQUARED-OFF
Woven, triple weave; 4-
rod coils, packing on
corners, cane-wrapped
handle, rattan; 10 by 17½
by 10 inches. Photo by
John C. Keys.

C

Diane Deyo
SOLITUDE
Coiled; raffia, cherry; 8
by 19 by 8 inches.

D

Anita Bowman
FEATHER MY NEST
Woven; wild vines; 18 by
20 by 4 inches.

*My work is more influenced
by nature and the wild
materials I gather than by
anything else. My most
successful baskets are made
when I let the wild materials I
gather dictate the type of basket
I will weave instead of having
a particular basket in mind
and trying to find the
materials to weave it.*

B

C

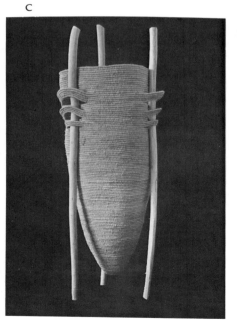

D

A
Douglas Eric Fuchs
FOREST GROUP
Woven (double weft),
twined; raffia, flat and
round reed, bamboo,
grapevine, manila rope,
rolled paper, leather,
twigs; tallest - 72 by 16
by 16 inches. Photo by
Doug Long.

B
Kathleen Curtis
SHIFTING SANDS
Coiled; raffia, fiber flex;
28 by 19 by 10 inches.

C
Dianne Stanton
COCOON
Hoop and rib basketry;
rattan, recycled World
War II dog sled hoops,
dyed with black walnut
hulls; 46 by 25 by 22
inches.

The hoop and rib technique
allows me to make a basket
structure out of almost any-
thing, whether I gather it in
the fields and woods or recycle
found objects.

A

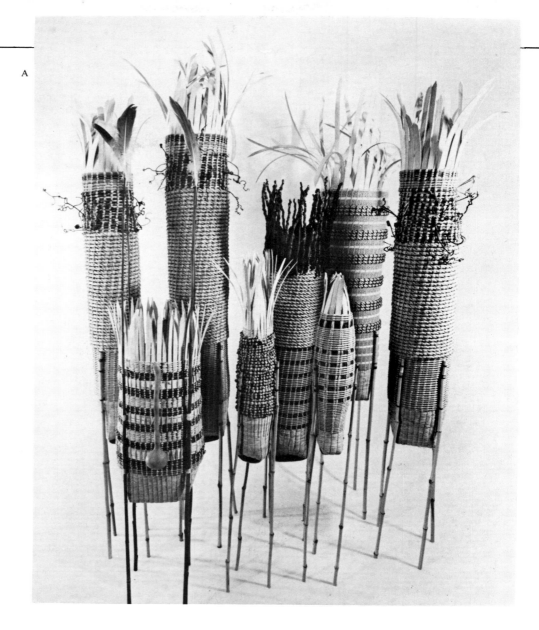

B

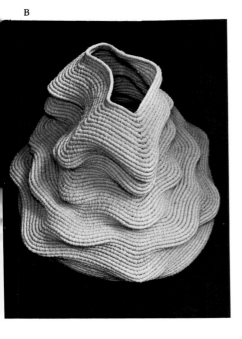

C

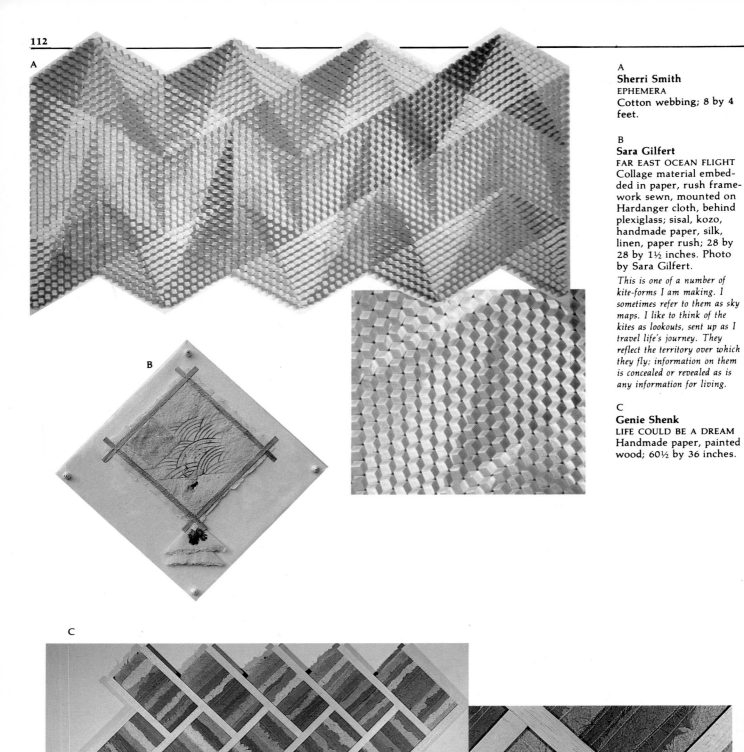

A
Sherri Smith
EPHEMERA
Cotton webbing; 8 by 4 feet.

B
Sara Gilfert
FAR EAST OCEAN FLIGHT
Collage material embedded in paper, rush framework sewn, mounted on Hardanger cloth, behind plexiglass; sisal, kozo, handmade paper, silk, linen, paper rush; 28 by 28 by 1½ inches. Photo by Sara Gilfert.

This is one of a number of kite-forms I am making. I sometimes refer to them as sky maps. I like to think of the kites as lookouts, sent up as I travel life's journey. They reflect the territory over which they fly; information on them is concealed or revealed as is any information for living.

C
Genie Shenk
LIFE COULD BE A DREAM
Handmade paper, painted wood; 60½ by 36 inches.

A

Shirley Venit Anger
THERE'S A GREAT
TENNIS BALL IN THE SKY
Embroidered; cotton
suede; 45 by 54 inches.

B

Jan Manley
CAVEAT EMPTOR
Machine embroidered,
hand stitched, appliqued,
stretched; poplin, calico,
rayon and cotton thread,
spray dye; 26 by 30
inches.

*At the time of this piece, I was
absorbed with doing portrait
"types" in fiber. The subject
here was a shady second-hand
sewing machine dealer from
whom I had bought a
"lemon"; thus, the "typecast"
study.*

C

Cynthia Nixon-Hudson
THE WAY TO DELOS
Pieced, appliqued with
ink-drawn passages;
cotton, voile; 42 by 28
inches.

*This piece, based on the myth
of the Greek sacred isles, uses
dolphins as mediators between
life and spirit and is about
death, transition, and spiritual
voyage. My work is often
concerned with symbolism and
myth as a way of passing on
knowledge of relationships
between nature and culture.*

A

B

C

A

B

C

A
Alicia Savery
MEMORIAL
Coiled; raffia, sisal,
bamboo; 45 by 8½ by 9
inches.

*Much of my work is inspired
by simple form in suspension.
The potential for movement,
the artifact as a once utili-
tarian object no longer in use
both form a base to work from.*

B
Margrit Schmidtke
UNTITLED III
Reed basket; 8 by 16
inches.

C
Shirley Spicher
A CRADLE FOR IVAN
Woven; wool, wild
grapevine, pheasant
feathers; 30 by 40 by 30
inches.

A
Barbara Cohen
UNTITLED
Woven, wrapped; linen; 6
by 21 by 5 inches.

B
Marla Mallett
PERPETUAL NOTION:
WITH BLACK
Woven; wool, acrylic; 43
by 43 by 2 inches. Photo
by Marla Mallett.

C
SISELLA
(Heidi Baumann)
THE PRISON IN ONESELF
Twined (personal tech-
nique); coconut fiber; 39
by 39 inches.

THE PRISON IN ONESELF
*has a passage, a little window
in the center of the work. That
open door is also in us: liberty,
silence, mysticism and
universe. People have to try
and find it and it will be freedom throughout.*

D
Ruth Geneslaw
RANDOM VARIATIONS
Wool knit tubing layered
and hand stitched on
stretched muslin; 72 by
72 by 3½ inches.

*This architectural wall relief
is particularly interesting to
me because I designed it so the
16 modules can be assembled
in many different configura-
tions, each time producing a
new design.*

A

B

C

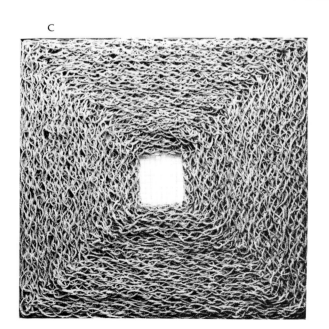

D

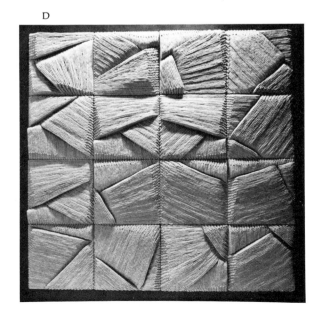

A

A
Sally Bailey
FLIGHT OF FANCY
Hooked; recycled wool
fabric, burlap; 38 by 35½
inches.

B
Margaret Cusack
PERRIER
Machine stitched,
appliqued, dyed; hand-
made lemon and lime
buttons; satin, silk, terry-
cloth, cotton, velvet; 20
by 28 inches.

*This piece was commissioned
for Perrier as a proposed
advertising poster. It was to
show that Perrier and fruit
juices are a good combination.
The poster was well-received
but ultimately not used as
intended.*

B

A
Colleen Christie-Putnam
UNTITLED
Cotton and abaca paper,
acrylic medium; 42 by 25
inches.

B
Jane Burch Cochran
FOR A WARRIOR'S WIDOW
Sewn, beaded; painted
canvas, fabric, yarn,
Xerox transfer, leather,
beads, metal locket; 13½
by 15 inches.

*The work involved in these
pieces is intricate and time-
consuming. The slow application of the beads allows time to
deliberate and change; and the
piece emerges slowly. The
content is from a past time
when the Indian culture
flourished. I have recomposed
these elements and combined
them with my own reflections
of an era I know only through
history.*

C
Jane Burch Cochran
RECEIVING THE NIGHT
VISION
Sewn, beaded; painted
canvas, Xerox transfer,
fabric, handmade paper,
beads, 17 by 18 inches.

A

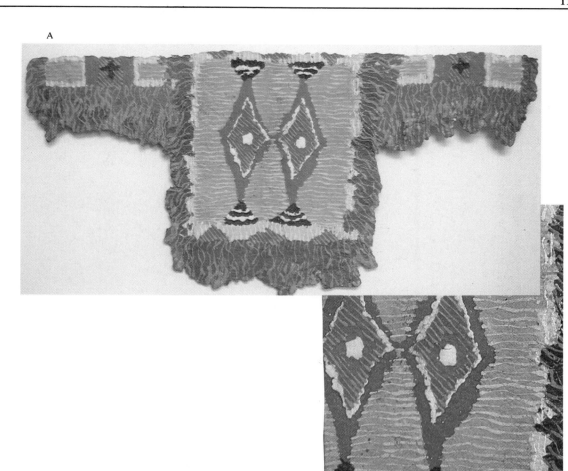

B

C

A

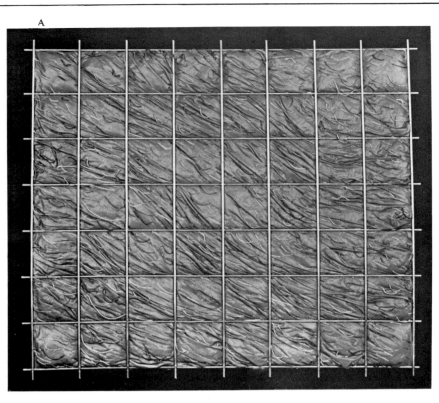

A
Kay Campbell
STRUCTURED REFLECTIONS
Mixed media; hand dyed
fabric and yarns, stitched;
mylar, rayon, metal; 30
by 33½ inches.

B
Katryna Hadley
JACKSON I
Machine knitted, fabric
backed and stitched; silk,
wool, cotton, rayon; 49½
by 64 inches.

JACKSON *is a modern, knit*
expression of the traditional
"log cabin" quilt.

B

A
Suellen Glashausser
DISHRAGS
Stitched, painted; tulle,
paint; 17 by 16 inches.

B
Louise Jamet
BOITE A COUTURE #4
Drawn, color Xeroxed,
embroidered, wrapped;
cotton, bamboo, colored
pencil, cotton thread; 30
by 30 inches.

C
Carol Baker
REMNANTS OF A
MATERIAL WORLD
Painted, stitched, padded
surface; tissue paper,
fabric, paint; 19½ by 5½
feet. Photo by David
Huron-Moore.

*The title has double meaning.
The triangle (matter trans-
forming into spirit) rises out of
the ashes of a material society;
the scraps on the surface I
collected while working as a
sewing machine operator in a
non-union garment factory.*

A

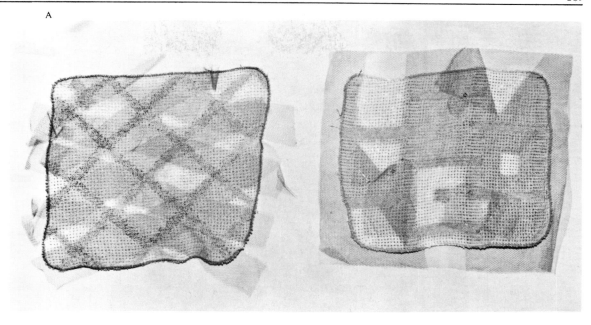

B

C

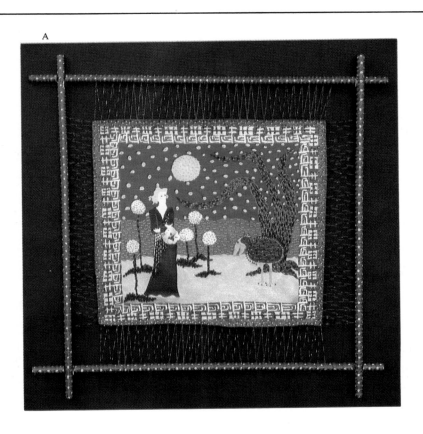

A

Jerry Stefl
SELENA SERENADING
THE ROC
Painted, beaded, em-
broidered; leather, beads,
wooden poles, embroid-
ery thread; 20 by 20
inches.

*This series of leather pieces is
based on historical precedents
of beaded leather work from
the Americas and Africa. The
images are gathered from geo-
graphical locations and
popular cultural history.*

B

Claire M. Starr
EIS AIONA I (IN ETERNITY)
Appliqued, stitched,
beaded; cotton, cotton/
polyester, metallic thread,
sequins; 24½ by 20.

*This piece represents forces in
the Universe from before time
and into eternity, although
they may become ragged and
tarnished with age. It departs
from traditional applique in
that the edges are left exposed
so that the raveling process
may continue with time.*

A
Jeannie Kamins
SATURDAY NIGHT AT
THE MOVIES
Appliqued; mixed fabrics;
45 by 32 inches.

B
Jeannie Kamins
THE BATHERS
Appliqued; mixed fabrics;
10 by 6 feet.

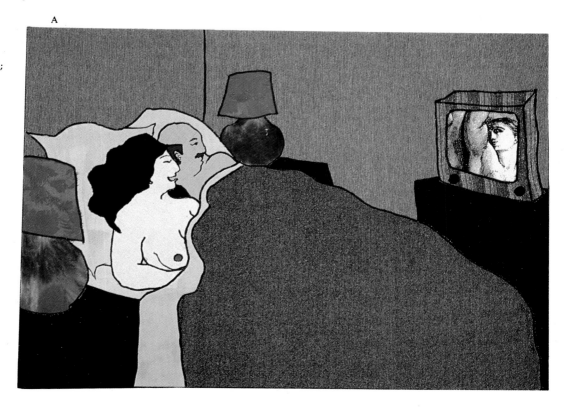

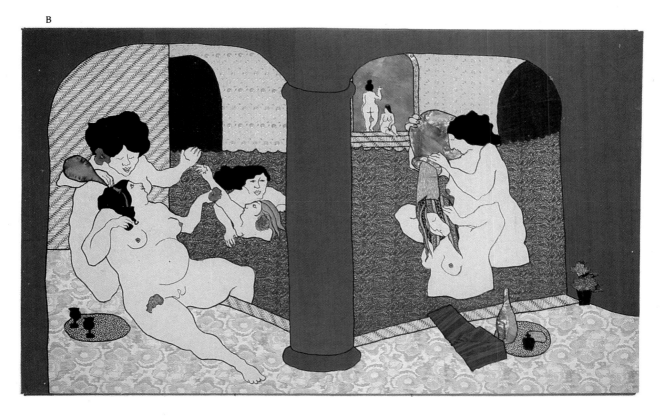

A

Douglas Eric Fuchs
CHEDIS 1-5
Woven (double weft),
twined; raffia, sea grass,
reeds, telephone wire,
acrylic paint; circum-
ference and height for
each piece - 56 by 47
inches, 47 by 51 inches,
25 by 39 inches, 60 by 41
inches, 40 by 40 inches.
Photo by Doug Long.

*These five pieces were inspired
by the temple spires of
Thailand called Chedis.*

B

Adrienne Diner
OMEGA
Hand painted, quilted,
mounted on plywood;
raw silk, metallic thread,
polyester fiberfill, ¼-inch
plywood; 12 by 8 feet.

*This piece was commissioned
for a residential environment
and was designed to work with
existing interior colors as well
as with the furnishings and
wall slats. The image for the
piece was designed with strong
horizontal graphic qualities so
continuity of image would not
be lost with the wrapping of
the fabric on the plywood as
well as the existing one-inch
space between the slats.*

A
Ellen Mears
HARLEQUIN'S DREAM
Felted, attached to canvas
backing; handmade felt;
54 by 174 by 3 inches.

B
Carol Jessen
SPECTRUM
Appliqued, pieced,
stitched; 16 by 17½
inches.

C
Karen Chapnick
NOW AND THEN
Hand dyed, braided; sisal;
20 by 6 feet. Photo by
Henri Robideau.

A

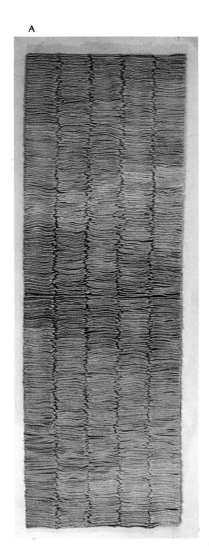

B

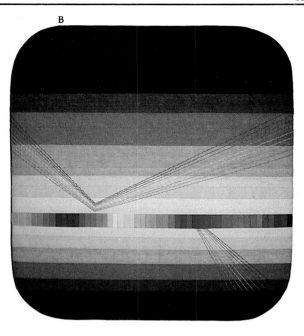

C

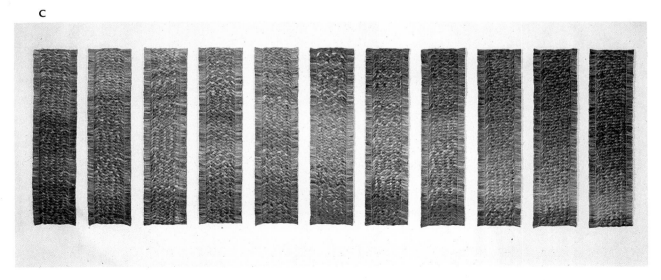

124

A
Ann Savageau
TURNING POINT:
CELESTIAL IMAGE
Individual technique, 364
felt rectangles hung on
wood lattice with pins;
felt, paint, dye; 48 by 78
inches.

B
Mary Towner
SUSPENDED ARCS
Machine felted; dyed
wool fleece; 65 by 45
inches.

C
**Marleah Drexler
MacDougal**
CHASM
Felted; handmade felt,
wool fleece, Ciba Acid
dye, Fiberglass screening;
64 by 60 inches.

A
Robert Burningham
CROSS
Embroidered, beaded;
silk, polyester, cotton,
rayon, metal threads,
beads, copper wire; 39½
by 42 inches.

B
Robert Hillestad
LES MANNEQUINS
Appliqued, stitched; wool
and silk fabric; silk
thread; 18 by 16 inches.

A
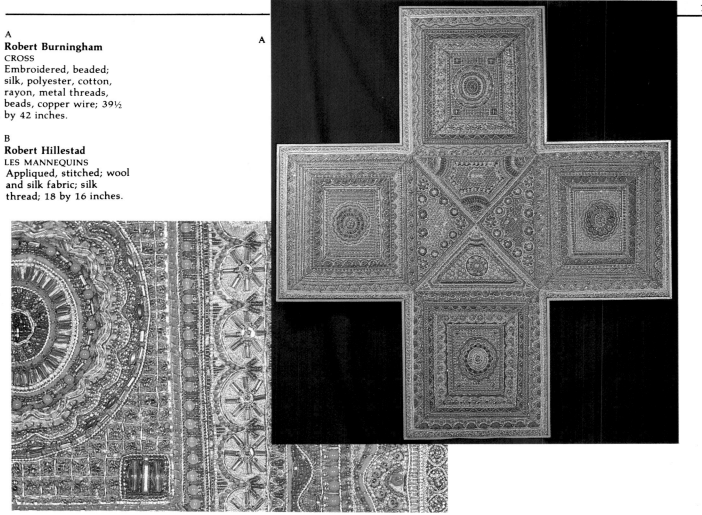

B

A

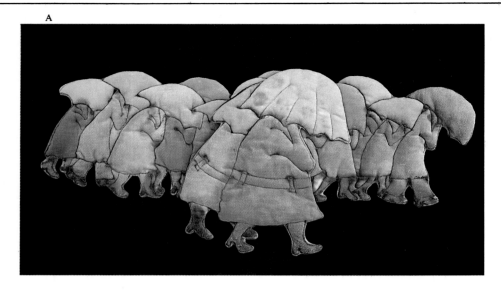

A
Cindy Hickok
TWENTY PERCENT
CHANCE OF RAIN
Trapunto; fiber reactive
dye, cotton velveteen,
polyester fiberfill; 20 by
12 inches.
*When the morning newscaster
predicted 20% chance of rain
on the day of a major flood in
Houston, I felt compelled to do
this piece.*

B
Carol Nash
LILLIES
Stitched; cotton fabric,
polyester batting, wire;
45 by 33 by 7 inches.

C
Jean Carlson Masseau
PASTURE PUZZLE I
Handsewn, appliqued,
trapunto; velveteen,
satin, suede; 45 by 15 by
2 inches. Photo by Erik
Borg.

B

C

A
Charlotte Amalie
Purrington
THE GOOD RETURN
Embroidered, hand
quilted, wax resist;
cotton surface, polyester
batting, cotton em-
broidery floss; 27 by 18
inches.

This was designed for a baby's
room and was presented as a
gift from a grandparent to a
new, first grandchild.

B
Salley Mavor
CROQUET GAME
Appliqued, embroidered,
relief sculpture; fabric,
ribbon, paper flowers,
wire, wood, thread; 15 by
20 inches.

A

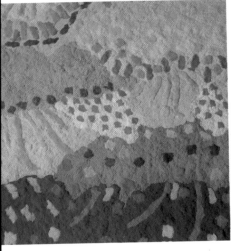

B

C

A
Connie Miller
ROW BY ROW
Handmade paper; cotton,
bamboo; 56 by 51 inches.

*My concerns in this series are
with landscape imagery and
Fauvist color. Having begun
as a painter, I use paper as a
painter does paint.*

B
Rowen Schussheim
COLLAGE IV
Felted, stitched; rayon,
silk, wool, handmade felt;
4 by 8 feet.

C
Phoebe Gunn
EVENTAIL V
Felted; fleece, dye,
thread; 23 by 22 inches.

A

Kathy Constantinides
TIDAL OCCLUSION I
Sewn, torn layers; Pellon, metal, thread; 5 by 5 feet.

The dialogue is between inner and outer, private and public space. Tension and energy connect the two.

B

Jane Rademacher
UNTITLED
Felted, tapestry construction; handmade felt; 16 by 20 inches.

C

Anne O'Leary
VISUAL PROGRESSION OF TIME INVOLVING THE ELEMENTS
Newspaper, cotton, Peter Collingwood's double corduroy; 60 by 50 inches.

This piece involves the effects of time and change on newspaper. It is exciting to watch the piece change in color and its physical make-up. There are so many elements involved in the build-up and breakdown of paper.

D

Kay Campbell
STRATA
Mixed media; hand dyed fabric and yarns, stitched and combined with metal wire screen; mylar, rayon, wire screening; 32 by 38 inches.

A

B
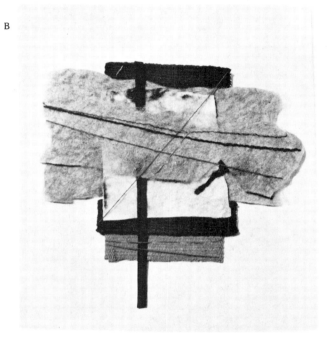

C
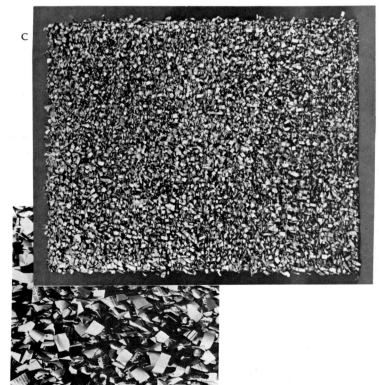

D
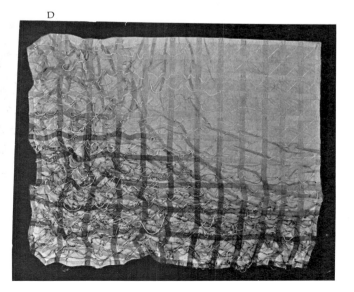

A

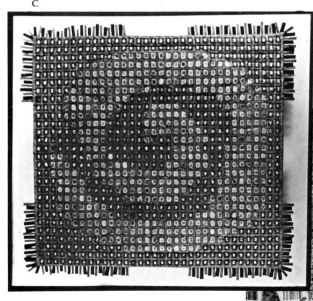

A
Karen Meyerhoff
UNDERWATER PARADE OR
JACQUES COUSTEAU
ON THE SONY
Felted; handmade felt
using hand dyed wool; 5
by 7 feet. Photo by
Sharon Miller.

B
Sharron Parker
DAYBREAK GRID
Felted, inlaid woven
areas; handmade felt,
wool, mohair, other
fibers; 53 by 40 inches.

C
Carol Baker
GROSS NATIONAL
PRODUCT
Appliqued, painted, dyed,
tuft quilted, stitched;
paper, plastic, acrylic
paint, dye; 91 by 94
inches. Photo by Bob
Shell.

*This piece uses Universal
Product Codes in a statement
about mechanized man.*

B

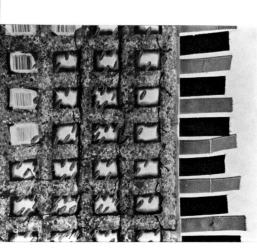

C

A
Stacy Digiovanni Koehler
FLIGHT
Handmade paper, produced in panels using a resist technique to provide flaps; 36 by 36 inches.

I was concerned with the movement of air/wind as evidenced by what is carried by the currents with the collision of normally unseen forces.

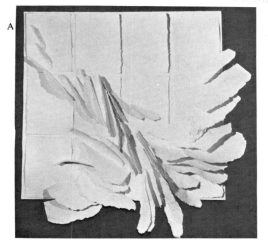

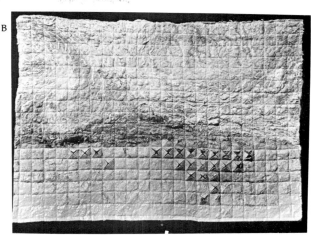

B
Stephanie Grubbs
CHARTING THE MORNING
Felted, handmade paper; wool, rayon, silk, flax paper, acrylic; 44 by 32 inches. Photo by Rod Grubbs.

Many of my works illustrate the catching of a small moment in beauty in a net, a chart or graph. Just as this idea is preposterous, so do the fibers escape from my stitched nets and graphs.

C
Linda Fouts
KEEPSAKE X1
Handmade paper; 60 by 36 inches.

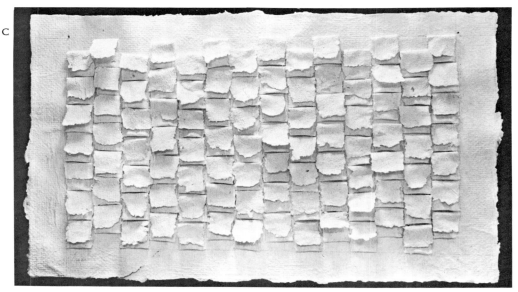

D
Holley Junker
DIVIDE! SUBDIVIDE!
Paper, organdy, rubber stamps, dye; 31½ by 50½ inches.

I was invited to enter an art show and the theme was maps of Sacramento (California). This piece speaks to growth and the filling of space with houses.

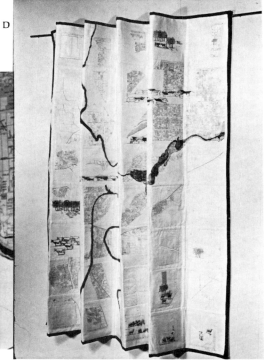

A

B

C

A

Deirdre Brocklebank
CANBERRA. THE NATIONAL
CAPITAL, 1982
Handknitted (picture
knitting); handspun and
crocheted wool, metal
support rods; 42 by 50
inches.

B

Linda Lee Ominsky
INCREASE, MULTIPLY &
COVER THE EARTH – THE
FISHES (GENESIS–THE
5TH DAY)
Appliqued, stitched,
handsewn; mohair,
cashmere, chinchilla, felt,
ultrasuede, thread, yarn;
53 by 54 inches.

*In Genesis, God created all the
animals on the fifth day. I
chose to illustrate the fishes
using repetition and variation
of color, shape and texture. On
the central earth, the land
seems to recede and the seas
stand out to emphasize the
importance of the fishes and of
the waters of the world. I
wanted to convey my plea for
clean and unpolluted seas and
my wish that the fishes will
increase and multiply as stated
in Genesis.*

C

Bettina Maylone
MEME DANS SA CUISINE
Embroidered, appliqued;
cotton, beads, metallic
threads, veil material,
wool; 26 by 23 inches.

*I enjoy designing things that
"work" and that have a sense
of humor, too. I got the idea
for this piece from looking at
the jars where I keep my silks
and beads.*

A

Robin Becker
PORTRAIT OF A GREEK
VILLAGE - WHEAT HARVEST
Mixed media, photography on silk embedded
into hand molded paper,
straw woven fragments;
34 by 21 inches.

B

Jennifer Holdham
MACINTOSH MOP CAP
RACE NO. 2
Machine appliqued;
cotton, cotton blends; 53
by 34 inches.

C

Therese May
DONNY'S PET HORSE
Stitched, painted; fabric,
acrylic paint, 33 by 32
inches.

D

Linda Lee Ominsky
HAPPY BIRTHDAY
PHILADELPHIA
Hand and machine sewn,
appliqued, stitched; wool,
synthetic fabric, mohair,
fake fur, felt; 44½ by
43½ inches.

*To commemorate the 300th
year since Philadelphia's birth,
I made this wall hanging of
William Penn, the founder of
Philadelphia and William
Green, the current Mayor.*

A

B

C

D

A

B

A
Cathy Smith
SITTING HIGH ON
MY CHAIR
Machine stitched, quilted,
appliqued; cotton muslin,
antique quilt made of
cotton on wood backing;
34 by 50 inches.

B
Susan Brotchie
SUNDAY'S CHILD
OR TREE OF LIFE
Stuffed, hand quilted and
embroidered child;
machine pieced, patch-
work blocks; 20½ by 30
by 2 inches.

C
Karyl Sisson
PUTTING MYSELF OUT
THERE I
Stitched assemblage; old
fabrics, old family photos,
plastic beads, color
Xerox; 20 by 20 inches.

D
Joyce Marquess Carey
TESSELATED TWILL
Appliqued, machine
stitched; cotton; 6 by 8
feet.

C

D

A
Barbara Macey
WAVE 2, JORDANVILLE
CUTTING
Pieced, patchwork;
cotton, synthetic fabric;
102 by 65 inches.

*This piece was inspired by
rock in a railway cutting near
my home and is part of a
series about pattern with
curved shapes.*

B
Elsa Waller
PIROUETTE
Folded, dipped, plaited,
painted; cotton webbing,
Createx dye; 60 by 39 by
4 inches.

*I find working with the
webbing and dyes in connec-
tion with my weaving and
plaiting techniques has opened
up a whole new dimension for
me.*

C
Pam Castano
WHOOSH
Appliqued; cotton and
cotton/polyester on
canvas; three panels: 42
by 60 inches each. Photo
by Doug Jones.

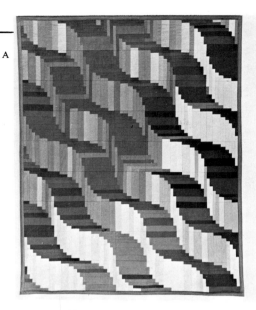

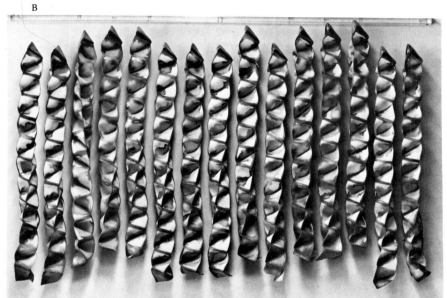

A

B

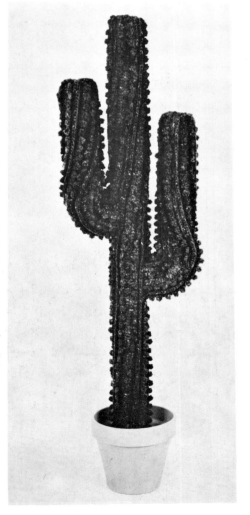

C

A
Felix and Emma Senger
ICON OF THE HOLY
SHROUD
Appliqued, machine
embroidered; man-made
and natural fiber fabrics;
60 by 36 inches.

*This was made for the private
chapel of the Most Reverend
Michael J. Dudick, Bishop of
Passaic, New Jersey.*

B
Janice Oelberg
SAGUARO CACTUS
Crocheted, dyed; cotton,
handspun wool; 2 by 7
feet.

C
Roslyn Logsdon
DAYTONA BEACH 1949
Hooked; woolen fabric
strips, burlap backing; 38
by 25 inches.

*My wall hangings are my
paintings dealing with the
past. The colors used are soft
colors to emphasize the softness
of memories. I feel these images
belong to everyone's past.*

A

Pamela Jean Burg
HOOD
Pieced, appliqued; cotton rag paper; 28 by 37 inches.

The intention of my work is to make a statement which employs a reference to the textile arts and my personal association with interior spaces. The fabric is constructed of inexpensive paper and acetate, materials commonly utilized for contemporary disposable containers. The imagery of the fabric incorporates bold patterns and subtle suggestions of architectural spaces.

B

Aya Kimura
SQUARES
Hooked process; hand dyed wool; 36 by 36 inches.

C

Annie Dempsey
PAKISTAN WEAVE
Woven crochet; cotton, artificial silk; 36 by 65 inches.

D

Susanna Starr
SAGITTARIUS
Embroidered; silk and cotton thread on cotton; 12¾ by 18¾ inches.

A

B

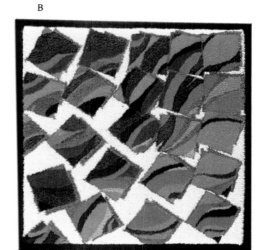

C

D

A

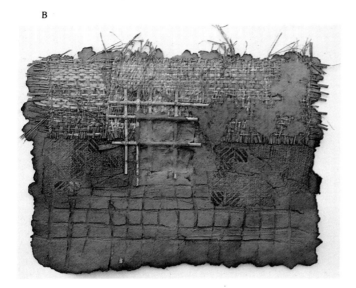

B

C

A
Janet Leszczynski
HIGHLIGHTED SQUARE
Embroidered; cotton
thread on silk.

*My imagery is composed of
geometric forms which on a
personal level symbolize the
stringent structures of my life.
I acknowledge this rigidity, yet
seek to modify it in my work
through the use of subtle
structural interruptions and
color gradations. My desire is
to provide an image which
encourages a peaceful and
beautiful state of mind for
myself and the viewer.*

B
Barbara Fast
SHAMAN SHABONO
Mixed media, cast paper;
cotton, paper, mixed
fibers, acrylic stamping;
21 by 16 inches.

*Paper as a medium lends itself
easily to a creative approach
that is appealing to me, one
that offers a certain amount of
control but permits surprising
accidents. It is this element
that keeps the process
intriguing, even mysterious
and that, in turn, sometimes
suggests the mood or subject
matter of my pieces.*

C
Carmen Grier
GRAFFITI GRID
Folded, dyed, painted;
cotton canvas, rayon
yarn, acrylic paint; 69 by
44 inches.

*Currently, my emphasis is on
the development of a personal
language contained within a
formal structural system.
Included are graffiti-like
messages, letters and mementos
which are applied within a
grid system on dyed canvas.*

Lisa Hedstrom
UNTITLED
Resist dyed, shirred; silk.
Photo by Elaine Keenan.

A

A
Danica Eskind
HARLEQUIN T-TOPS
Photograms printed on
viscose rayon challis
using light sensitive dyes.
Photo by Joe A. Watson.

*In my work now, I am com-
bining man-made and natural
objects and am trying to
investigate both shadow effects
and the interplay of positive
and negative spaces. The type
of objects I use and their juxtaposition have also become more
important. My utmost concern
is still in integrating images,
fabric and final wearable
form.*

B
Diana Jahns
SPINNAKERS
Woven, ikat technique
with pieced applique;
cotton warp, silk and
cotton weft.

C
Lynda Dautenhahn
RUBY'S LIVING ROOM
Painted, drawn, quilted,
trapunto; satin acetate.

B

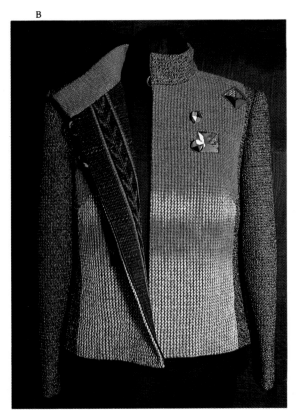

C

A
Susan D. Summa
SISTER MOON TUNIC
Loom knitted; cotton,
lurex. Photo by R. Faller.

B
Susan D. Summa
BEEHIVE COAT
Loom knitted; wool,
lurex.

*This coat was inspired by a
show the Renwick Gallery
(Washington, D.C.) had in
1981 about beehives.*

C
Sharon Robinson
RIDING COSTUME
Hand painted, quilted,
strip pieced, hand dyed;
silk pongee, polyester
batting.

D
Faye G. Anderson
RUBICS CUBE
Pieced, appliqued; cotton,
wool, metallic fabrics.

B

A

C

D

A

Beth Holyoke
Kelly Thomas
UNTITLED
Spray dyed; silk broad-
cloth.
Fabric designed and dyed by
Beth Holyoke, garment
designed and constructed by
Kelly Thomas.

B
ALICIA
BLOUSON TOP
Woven tapestry inlay at
neck, knitted cuffs and
waistband; silk blends on
cotton warp.

C
Erin Bowker
MYSTICAL IRIS
Embroidered; cotton floss
on cotton velveteen.

B

C

A

Chris and Jacquelyn Faulkner
NAUTILUS
Pieced, quilted; cotton, acetate, cotton/polyester.

B

Jo Ann Giordano
COSMIC FANTASY JACKET
Silk-screen printed on silk, handmade frog closures. (Folkwear Chinese Jacket pattern)

Clothing has the potential to change the wearer's mood: to elevate the spirits, to amuse, to create magic. I would hope that my garments serve a similar function.

C

Susanna E. Lewis
FLIGHT PATH
Machine knitted, crocheted trim; wool yarn.

This was knit in a variety of jacquard techniques to produce sculptured fabrics in relief.

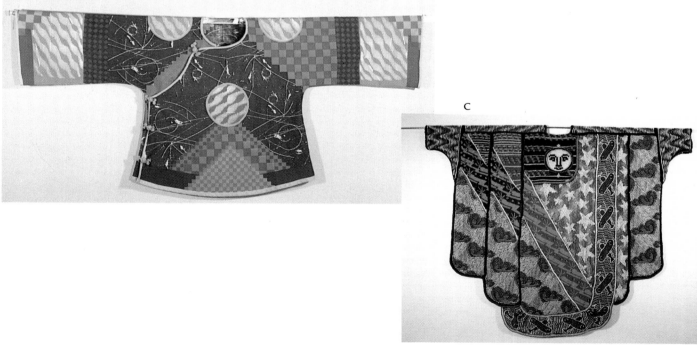

A

A
Lisa Hedstrom
UNTITLED
Resist dyed; silk crepe.
Photo by Elaine Keenan.

B
Ann Jean Welch
HOMAGE TO KLIMT
Batiked; silk crepe,
aniline dye. Photo by
Schecker Lee.

*At least part of my knowledge
of and about tjanting technique comes from my
experience of living and
working in the batik quarter of
Jogakarta in Java, Indonesia.
Unlike the modern Indo-
nesians, however, I never paint
on the dye, I fully submerge
the whole cloth, often as much
as 12 to 20 times, to get the
desired color combinations.*

B

A
Mickey Nushawg
TRIBUTE TO THE WOMEN PAINTERS OF MITHILA
Loom knitted; cotton.
Photo by John Spence.

This Birdseye Jacquard (double bed technique) is inspired by the designs in the saris painted in the traditional manner of Mithila women and passed down from generation to generation. Mithila is now part of the Bihar state in eastern India.

B
Pamela Wiley
POEM PAPERS & MAGIC CHARMS
Direct dyed with wax resist, painted on silk; Procion dye.

C
Shirley J. Fomby
SERENDIPITY
Stripple quilted, machine pieced, trapunto; silk, cotton batting, cotton/ polyester inner lining.

The jacket contains at least a million strippled quilting stitches which produced a marvelous effect, unobtainable in any other way. Thus, the name SERENDIPITY.

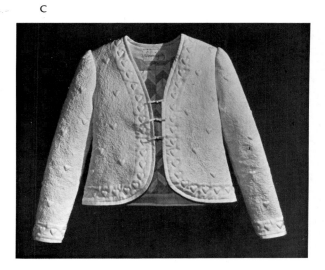

A

B

C

D

A
Holly Brackmann
STRIPED COTTOLIN JACKET
Woven with 12-harness warp face and weft face broken twill on rear of fabric.

B
Kathy Edelman Hutchinson
IKAT WRAP ROBE
Woven, warp ikat, resist tied and dyed; silk noil warp, cotton weft, hand dyed silk fabric sash and bindings, cotton fabric lining.

C
Lyn Carter
EVENING IN SPACE
Silk and nylon fabrics stuffed with kapok welting.

D
Elizabeth Garver
SHIRT SERIES #1
Machine appliqued; dyed silk pongee, silk noil.

A
Ann King
UNTITLED
Quilted, embellished;
cotton satin, glass beads.

B
Ann King
UNTITLED
Machine quilted, beaded;
cotton satin, glass beads.

C
Diane Ruble
NORTH SHORE JACKET
Machine pieced and
quilted (Seminole and
strip piecing techniques);
wool, cotton corduroy
lining, polyester batting.

D
Janet Higgins
ART NOUVEAU VEST
Silk-screen printed,
machine quilted, hand
beaded, hand couched;
cotton, beads, metallic
thread.

A

B

C

D

A

B

C

D

A
Janice Oelberg
TIBETAN COAT #2
Crocheted, dyed; hand-spun wool with rayon chenille and lurex accents.

B
Mary Ann Clayton
VEST
Woven (shaped on the loom), crocheted ruffle, braided belt; hand dyed cotton, chenille.

C
Jorie Johnson
PLAITED BAND VEST
Plaited, sewn; wool.
Photo by Jon Grass.

D
Lucy Matzger
Arlene Wohl
UNTITLED
Woven tapestry; wool, cashmere.

Arlene Wohl designs and weaves the fabric. Lucy Matzger interprets the fabric and designs the final garment. Although the collaboration is often inevitable, we allow each other complete autonomy in our separate crafts.

A
Pat Richardson
GREY BROWN CAPE
Woven, couched lines;
wool, pearl cotton.

B
Debby Pizur
UNTITLED
Crocheted; flat rayon
chenille yarn.

C
Laura J. Brookhart
SEASCAPE VEST
Polished cotton, silk
blends.

*This is my own version on the
tabard vest. The solid front/
back surfaces lend themselves
to endless exploration of color
and surface design.*

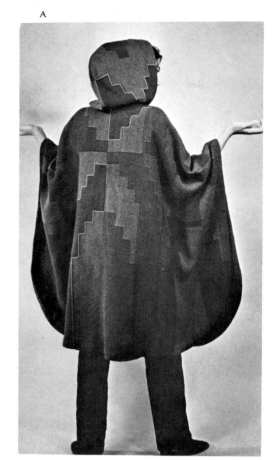

A

B

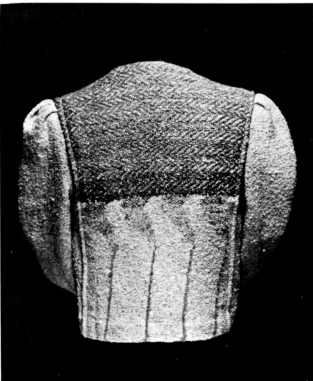

A
Sonja Saar
FUZZY THING
Hand-loomed, handknit-
ted and woven; mohair,
vegetable ivory buttons.

B
Carol Van Heerden
GRID JACKET
Woven, silk-screened
warp, embroidered;
cotton, Procion dye.

C
Rose Kelly
FOR ARTISTS WHO
HAVEN'T ANY HEAT
IN THEIR STUDIOS #2
Hand painted, stamped;
cotton long johns,
Versatex dye.

*I made a series of hand painted
and eraser stamped long johns
as a humorous digression. All
of the artists that I know work
diligently in unheated,
uncomfortable studio spaces. I
thought it would be great fun
if they could be all snugly
attired in stamped long johns.*

D
Cross/Lindsay
UNTITLED
Woven tapestry; cotton,
linen, silk, rayon.

*Cross/Lindsay is the combined
talent of a painter and a textile
artist.*

A

Ruth Fash
TAPESTRY MONTAGE IX
Woven, quilted; velvet,
satin, ribbon, bone
ornaments.
*Designed by Ruth Fash, woven
by Fran Rutkovsky.*

B

Linda Moore Durston
Prisca Mader
BLACK OVERLAY DRESS
Woven (Theo Moorman
technique variation);
rayon, linen, silk lining.

C

Shirley J. Fomby
COLLECTION ONE
Machine stitched labels,
hand quilted; wool
gabardine, polyester
batting.

D

Joan Wortis
UNTITLED
Woven; hand dyed wool.

*Arising from my work as a
dancer, I am concerned with
the drape and flow of the cloth
on the body and with a
symmetry in the design of the
cloth itself.*

A

B

C•

D

152

A

B

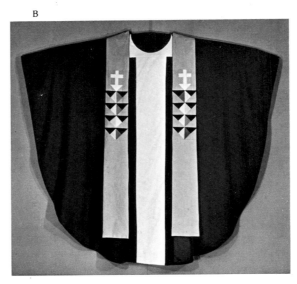

C

D

A
Mary Rawcliffe Colton
AND THERE APPEARED TO
THEM TONGUES AS OF
FIRE . . . ACTS 2:3
Woven, painted warp;
cotton, silk, rayon, linen.

B
Elaine Plogman
GREEN CHASUBLE
AND STOLE
Machine pieced; cotton,
blends.

C
Linda Lochmiller
THREE DRESSES FOR THE
JUDGES OF EMOTION
Appliqued with cotton on
cotton canvas. Photo by
Roger Huebner.

*The dresses were designed from
the pattern making stage to
carry applied symbols which
can be interpreted and even
read. Inspiration was drawn
from such diverse sources as
Emile Zola, Marianne Faith-
ful and my own personal
experiences.*

D
Conni Eggers
FESTIVAL CHASUBLE
Thai silk, silk linen, silk
satin, velveteen. Photo by
Eric Long.

A
Maria Da Conceicao
UNTITLED
Hand stitched; pure silk.

B
Peggy Kondo
UNTITLED
Woven; handspun and
dyed cotton.

A

B

A

John Marshall
CRANES AND IRIS
Hand dyed, rice paste
resist; silk noil, silk
habotai. Photo by Tom
Gibson.

*The entire piece is constructed
from three pattern pieces: right
side, left side and collar from
remnants. Tsutsugaki and
Katazome resist dye methods
were used. The entire piece
represents the grace and
inviting flight of warmth as
spring comes to the world.*

B

Laurence Brun
BLUE ILLUSION JACKET
Hand felted, hand dyed,
hand pieced; wool felt,
cotton lining.

C

Judith Stein
JACKET
Dyed, painted, quilted;
cotton, polyester batting.
Photo by Joe Watson.

A
Valerie Clausen
UNTITLED
Moccasin with hand-
woven shaft in
Norwegian Krokbragd
design; wool, sheepskin,
pigskin suede, cowhide.

B
Emmie Howard
FANTASY BOOTS
Knitted boot covers over
down booties; rayon
chenille with alpaca/
mohair lining.

C
Doris Louie
UNTITLED
Woven; wool weft,
cotton warp; bag - 11 by
11 by ½ inches,
checkbook - 4 by 8 by ½
inches, coin purse - 4 by
5 by ½ inches. Photo by
Pat Berrett.

D
Norma Minkowitz
ARE WE A PAIR?
Crocheted; synthetics,
cotton.

A

B

C

D

A

A
Judith Content
SILK COAT
Collage of hand dyed silks done in the traditional Japanese boumake technique, pieced and quilted with accents of trapunto; silk (raw silk, pongee, Thai, taffeta, China and satin), cotton/polyester batting, silk and polyester thread.

I design garments to reflect a mood, a season, a dream or a memory. They seem to unfold as they are dyed and pieced, sometimes reflecting my mood or the weather, other times with an instinct of their own.

B
Naomi Goto
SLEEVELESS COAT-OYAKO LIONS
Hand dyed silk chiffon, quilted onto silk noil lining, piped with silk habotai, shirred bodice.

Traditional Japanese designs and techniques have been used in producing contemporary one-of-a-kind wearable art. Design and color requests are presented along with sketches of garment designs to dyer John Marshall. The dyer hand dyes the fabrics using all natural dyes. Katazome and Tsutsugaki rice paste resist dyeing techniques are used.

B

A
Elizabeth Garver
BLUE PLEATED JACKET
Sixteen-harness satin
weave; cotton, dyed silk
pongee.

*In creating wearables, I am
interested in developing a
dialogue between garment and
participant that can broaden
and energize their combined
visual relationship.*

B
Doris Louie
UNTITLED
Woven tapestry; wool
weft, cotton warp, suede
binding, antique Navajo
silver button. Photo by
Pat Berret.

*I am most concerned in offer-
ing a well-made, well-designed
article for everyday use -
showing that art can be made
more a part of our daily lives
than normally thought.*

A

B

A

B

C

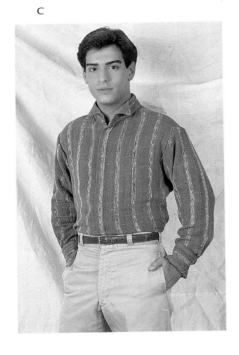

D

E

A
Marcia Phillips
JACKET
Woven tapestry, hand dyed; silk, rayon, ribbon.

B
Judith Kidd
CLOUD 9
Woven (ikat technique), tabby weave structure; cotton, pewter button on skirt.

C
Judith Kidd
MAN'S SHIRT
Woven (ikat technique), tabby weave structure, solid color in huck weave structure; cotton, antique mother-of-pearl buttons.

I feel there is a lack in hand-woven clothes for men. My man's shirt is geared to contemporary fashion with a wing collar and fly front.

D
Mary Rodgers
UNTITLED
Woven, ikat; pure wool. Photo by Sterling Ward Photographic Design.

E
Joan Wortis
UNTITLED
Woven; mohair, wool, cotton, rayon.

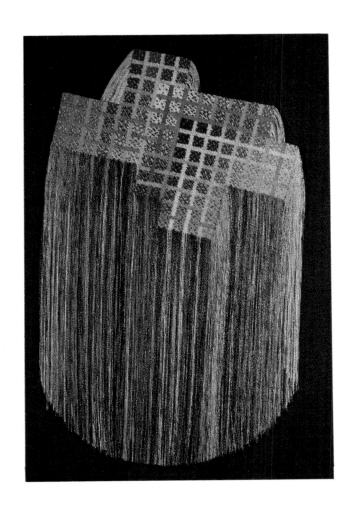

Diane Itter
TRIPLE GRID OVERLAP
Knotted; linen; 10 by 16
inches. Photo by David
Keister.

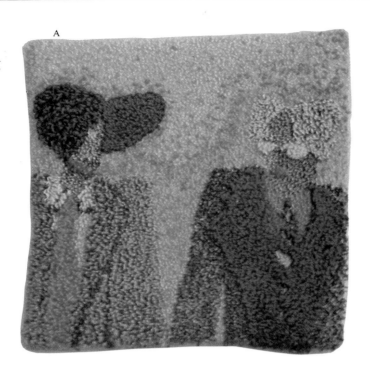

A

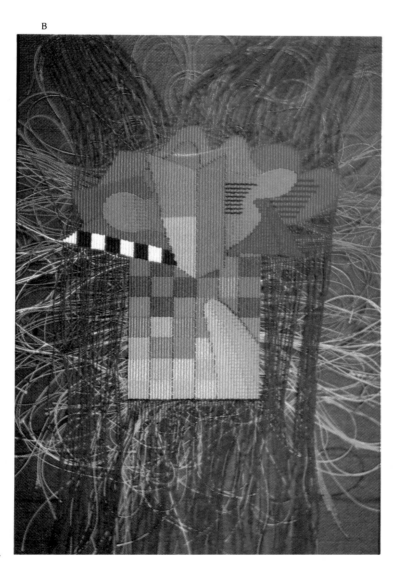

B

C

A
Connie M. Lehman
FLAM BOYS I
Igolochkoy (Russian
needlepunch); silk, cotton
thread on silk; 3¾ by 3¾
inches.

B
Susan L. Hoover
UNTITLED TREE FORM
Woven tapestry; silk sew-
ing thread; 3⅛ by 3¼
inches.

*Since moving to the plains of
Colorado, I have been working
in the miniature small scale.
The space here is enormous
and any growth of trees is
precious. A person is so small
in this environment. I am
intrigued and in awe of the
elements and my pieces portray
this relationship.*

C
Susanna Starr
WOMAN
Embroidered; cotton
thread on cotton; 9 by
10¼ inches.

A
Elizabeth Byrd
UNTITLED
Woven construction,
embroidered, dyed,
pieced; silk and cotton
thread, Procion dye,
cotton sateen; 4 by 6
inches.

B
Cynthia Laymon
DUNE PLANES I
Woven, drawn; wool,
colored pencils; 11 by 14
inches.

C
Renie Breskin Adams
WEATHER AFFECTS
PATTERN
Stitched; cotton sewing
threads; 4 by 3½ inches.

A

B

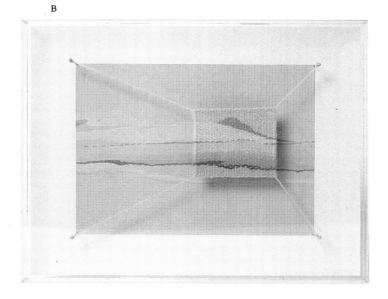

C

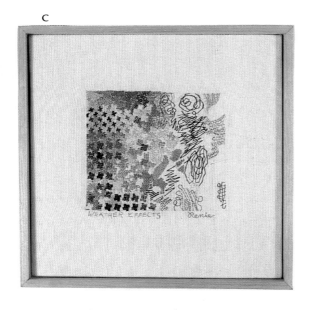

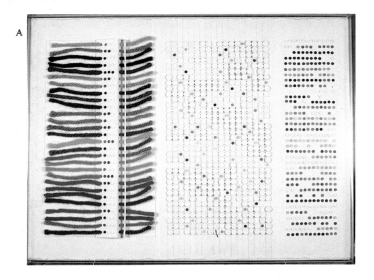

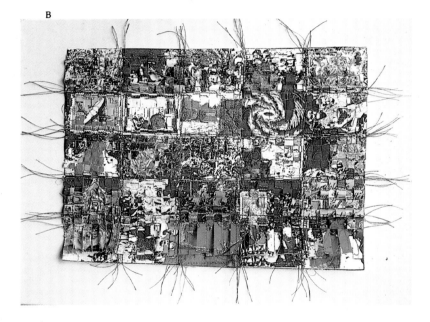

A
Cynthia Laymon
COLOR CARD 13
Collage; wool fibers, paper; 14 by 11 inches.
The color cards project the image of readable systems. The idea of a visual information system came from actual sample cards sent out by fiber supply companies.

B
Peggy Moulton
PICTURES PLAITED
Plaited; color Xerox, fabric; 9 by 12 by 2 inches.
First, I make a collage, then I color Xerox the collage. I applique fabric onto the Xerox with machine stitching. Next, I plait the two copies together, raising portions and pinning them. The pins become an important part of the design.

C
Tommye McClure
THEY FLOAT
Plain weave of machine stitched, painted paper; Inko dye, watercolor; 12¾ by 9¼ inches. Photo by M. Holmes/Dallas.

D
Elizabeth Aralia
KUAN
Raffia, handmade paper, silk, acrylic paint; 12 by 13 by 8 inches.

A

John L. Skau
LITTLE BOXES
Plaited; paper, ink; 4¼,
2¼, 1, ½ inches
respectively.

*My cubes often serve as a
metaphor for the various
processes of life. The
genealogy is clear in* LITTLE
BOXES *as one cube springs
forth from another.*

B

Lisa D'Agostino
RETURN OF THE COMET
Coiled; jute core, cotton
embroidery floss; ½ to
2½ by 8½ inches.

C

Lisa D'Agostino
SONGS FROM THE EARTH
Coiled; linen core, cotton
embroidery floss; ¾ to
2½ by 12 inches.

D

Michele Hament
TELEPHONE WIRE &
SISAL BASKET
Coiled (openwork coil-
ing); telephone wire,
sisal; 6 by 9 inches.

*I feel that baskets should be
functional as well as
aesthetically pleasing. I do not
want to limit myself to the use
of traditional materials and
enjoy exploring and blending
unusual materials and fibers.*

E

Kathleen M. Farling
MA BELL'S PERSIAN URN
Wrapped, coiled; plastic
coated telephone wire; 11
by 9 by 9 inches.

A

B
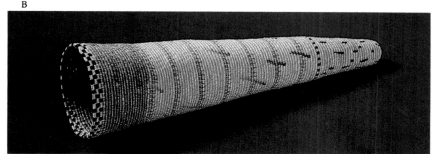

C
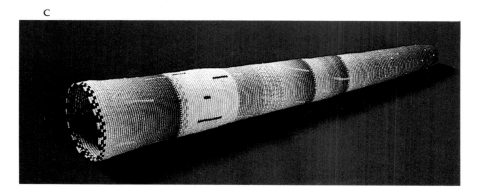

D

E
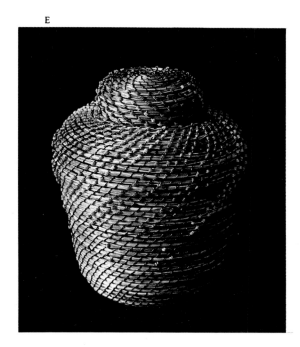

A

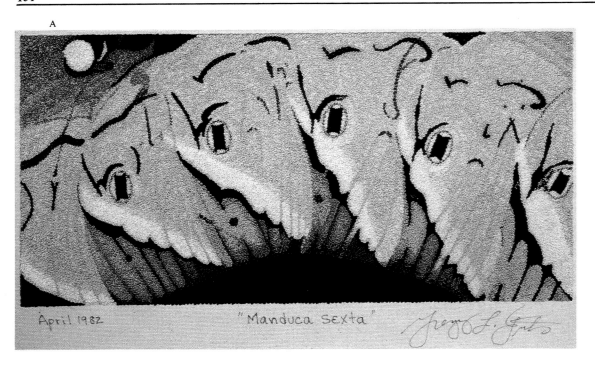

April 1982 "Manduca sexta"

A
Gregory L. Fiebing
MANDUCA SEXTA
Embroidered with french
knots; cotton embroidery
floss on cotton canvas; 10
by 5 inches.

B
Gregory L. Fiebing
CETHOSIA MYRINA
Embroidered with french
knots; cotton embroidery
floss on cotton canvas; 12
by 6 inches.

B

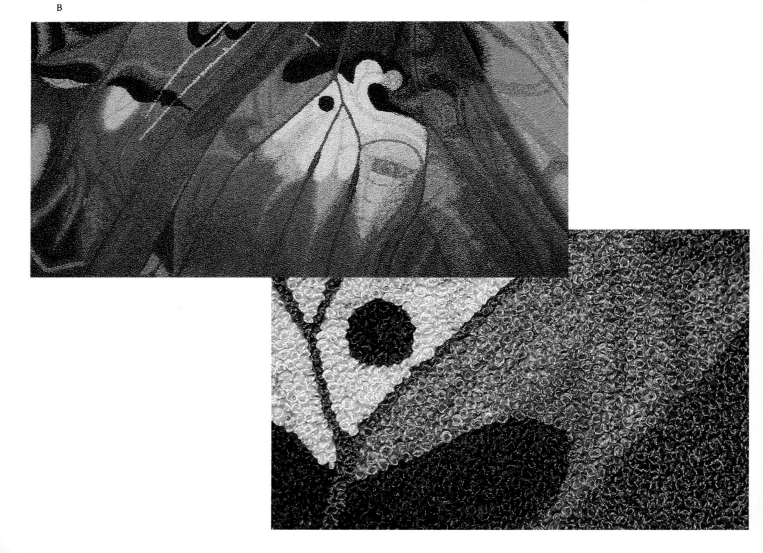

A
Mary Bero
MENAGERIE OUT WALKING
Embroidered; muslin,
cotton floss; 6 by 6
inches.

B
Mary Bero
UNVEILING SELF
Embroidered; muslin,
cotton floss; 5 by 7
inches.

*Through my artwork, I'm
constantly finding out more
about myself; exposing
insecurities and challenging
myself.* UNVEILING SELF *is a
tapestry painting about that
experience and growth with
"my family" watching and
cheering me on.*

A

B

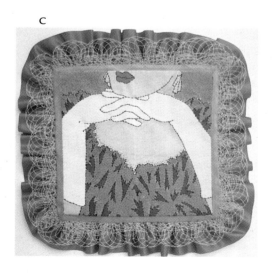

C

D

A
Joyce Marquess Carey
SELF PORTRAIT
Woven tapestry; rayon,
antique metallic thread;
11 by 14 inches.

B
Gray Griffith
SOUTHERNMOST HOUSE
Woven slit tapestry;
linen, hand dyed wool; 13
by 11 inches.
*This piece was inspired by a
special summer spent in the
Florida Keys.*

C
Michelle Morris
WAITIN' AT THE MOULIN
Embroidered, quilted,
printed; cotton, silk,
ribbon, plastic lace; 8 by
8 inches.

D
Ann L. Hense
EXTERIORS: II
Woven, machine appli-
qued; wool and cotton
yarn, thread; 7 by 12
inches.

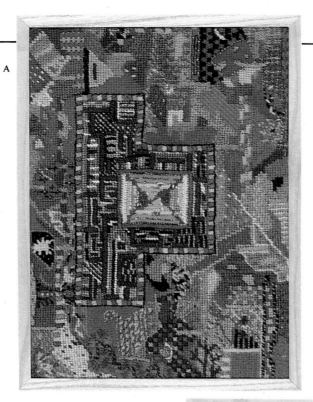

A

A

Paulis Neila Waber
UNTITLED
Embroidered; wool on
canvas; 11½ by 16 inches.

*The way I work on all of my
pieces is to sketch the broad
outlines of the piece onto the
canvas and then invent the
interiors as I go along. This
way I know my direction but
my interest is maintained by
not knowing how things will
turn out.*

B

Tracy A. Ruhlin
FORM AND LINE
MINIATURE #8
Double woven; Procion
dyed monofilament,
mylar, plastic tubing; 8
by 5½ inches.

*Twentieth century artists con-
cerned with movements of
geometric abstraction have
greatly influenced my double
woven bas-relief constructions.
Geometric rhythmic repetitions
of line, form and symmetry
emphasize the fact that the
piece exists for its own sake. I
feel my use of industrially
processed materials such as
Procion dyed monofilament,
mylar, lurex and plastic
tubing further emphasizes
impersonality and also speaks
of our contemporary culture.*

C

Mary Bero
PASSAGES
Painted, handmade paper;
acrylics, fabric, thread; 7
by 8⅝ inches.

B

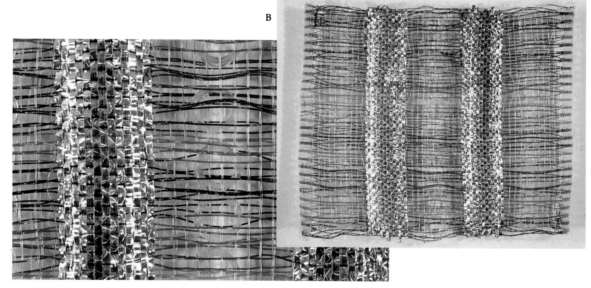

C

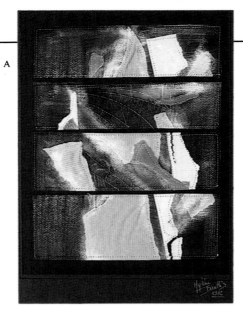

A

B

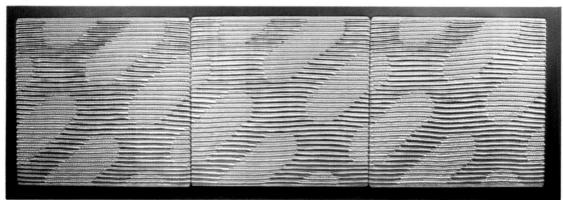

C

D

A
Mylene Daville
PINK ON BLACK
Sewn, painted paper
composition; craft paper,
thread, paint; 8½ by 11½
inches.

B
David C. Johnson
RED CROSS
Woven miniature
tapestry; cotton, linen; 20
by 9 inches.

C
Ruth Gowell
SPRING LATTICE
Woven, warp face weave
with twisted electrical
wire; hand dyed rayon,
electrical cord, nylon
monofilament, iridescent
mylar; 54 by 8 inches.

*This piece uses a technique I
have been experimenting with
which utilizes double electrical
wire. The wire is twisted in
areas and left straight in other
areas to develop designs. My
interest is in the light-reflective
qualities of the rayon and the
movement (vibration) created
by the shadows formed in the
twisted areas of the design.*

D
Judy Long Guerrero
LOLLIPOP ZEBRAS
Machine quilted, cyano-
type and kwik-print;
cotton and satin acetate;
32 by 12 inches.

*This piece, through the use of
color and pattern, represents
the whimsy and fantasy shared
with my children on our many
visits to the Phoenix Zoo.*

A
Beth Rakszawski
NOT A WEAK LINK
IN EVIDENCE
Wrapped; cotton; 9 by 10
by 2 inches.

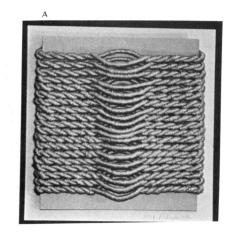

B
Linda H. Konya
TWO BOYS IN EDEN-
HVERAGERDI, ICELAND
Embroidered with needle-
lace and needle weaving;
cotton on linen, mirrors;
12½ by 9½ inches.

C
Jean Daveywinter
RANDOM MEMORIES
Assemblage set in plaster
including casts from
etching plates, stitched;
handmade paper, collage
materials, fabrics; 11 by
14 inches.

*In my recent work I have
related the way in which the
electronic memories of
computers respond to abstract
numbers and symbols with the
way in which the human
memory responds to the
ephemera of the past.*

D
Marcel Marois
WINTER GREY SKY
Woven tapestry, high
warp; natural wool, linen;
6½ by 6½ inches. Photo
by Yves Martin.

*The conception of my current
work is an interplay between
the structure and tapestry
image contributing sym-
bolically to the message of each
of them.*

E
Holley Junker
BEFORE GOODBYE
Embroidered; Xerox
transfer, silk; 10 by 10 by
1 inches (closed).

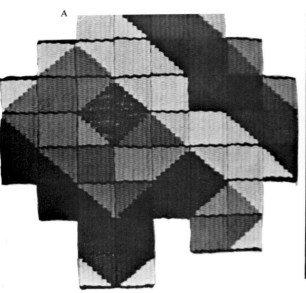

A

B

C

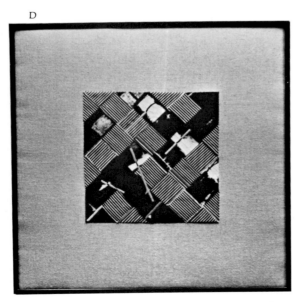

D

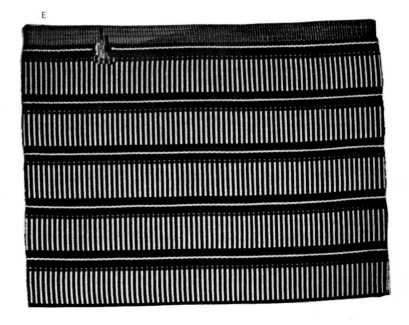

E

A
Ginger Luters
INTERFACE
Woven (slit tapestry technique); linen warp, cotton and rayon weft; 8 by 8 inches.

B
Terry Bryant Wise
GARDEN THROUGH AN OPEN WINDOW
Woven tapestry (Kilim); wool weft on linen warp; 13⅛ by 13½ inches.

C
Ruth Tanenbaum Scheuer
ABALONE
Woven, high warp tapestry; wool, silk, cotton; 14 by 11 inches. Photo by Doug Long.

D
Roxanne Kukuk
CONNECTED TISSUES #6
Machine stitched, plaited, appliqued; tied and bleached fabric, commercially printed fabric, cotton, cotton/polyester; 8¾ by 8¾ inches (unframed). Photo by J. Webster Vierow.

I like to contrast the regularity of the stripe against the softness and surprise which results when black fabric is tied and bleached.

E
David C. Johnson
MATCH STICK
Woven miniature tapestry; cotton, linen; 13½ by 11 inches.

A

Teresa Iversen
AS ALWAYS
Embroidered (back stitch); pearl cotton, wooden box; 8½ by 12 by 4½ inches.

B

April Hines
DAD
Woven tapestry; silk weft, cotton warp; 7 by 10 inches.

C

Claire E. Zerkin
DOUBLE WOVEN
PICTURE #2
Woven, double weave pick-up, ikat warp, some areas stuffed; cotton warp and weft, unspun wool, Pentel water color dye; 7 by 12½ inches.

D

Joyce Marquess Carey
8" X 10" GLOSSIES
Woven tapestry; rayon; 8 by 10 inches.

Photographs are so much a part of the way we all represent our work. They become almost as important as the fiber work they represent. These pieces are woven photographs of photographed weavings.

A

B

C

D
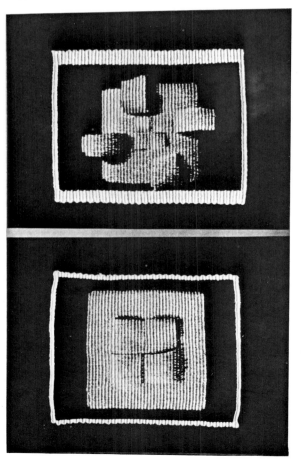

A

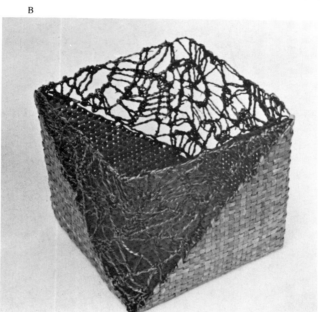

B

C

D

A
Jeanie Eberhardt
UNTITLED
Woven, wrapped; jute,
handspun mohair, cotton;
10 by 6 by 12 inches.

B
Marian Haley Beil
BASKET #6
Plaited, bobbin lace; nito,
palm leaf; 8¾ by 8¾ by
8¾ inches.

C
Gammy Miller
SCROLL BASKET
Coiled; waxed linen with
cinnamon bark; 4 by 3¼
by 4 inches. Photo by
Ken Kimerling.

*I am interested in making my
materials do things charac-
teristic of other media. In this
case, to build the hard-edged
forms that create an illusion of
permanence and solidity asso-
ciated more with clay than
with a soft material such as
linen.*

D
Sue Pierce
IRIS BOWL
Quilted; silk, synthetics,
polyester batting; 4 by 10
by 10 inches.

A

Carol Weingarten McComb
EARTH VESSEL
Handmade paper bowl, greased mold method; cotton, sawdust, steel wool, wax, twigs; 10 inches in diameter, 5 inches high.

This is part of a series inspired by a childhood fantasy of digging up ancient bowls.

B

Joan Hackley-McNeil
UNTITLED
Twined; paper fiber rush; 14 by 14 by 11 inches.

C

Jane Sauer
GATEWAY
Knotted waxed linen; 3½ by 11¾ by 3½ inches. Photo by Huntley Barad.

I intend to draw the observer into the piece as a participant by virtue of scale and attention to detail. The object should give one impression when seen as a whole and reveal something new when viewed closely.

D

Kathleen M. Farling
CONICAL CORE VESSEL
Knotted, coiled, wrapped; waxed linen, linen, copper wire; 9 by 15 by 15 inches.

A

B

C
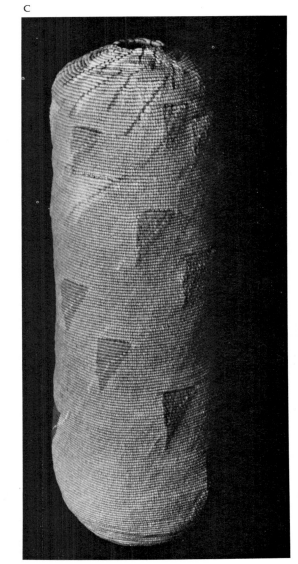

D
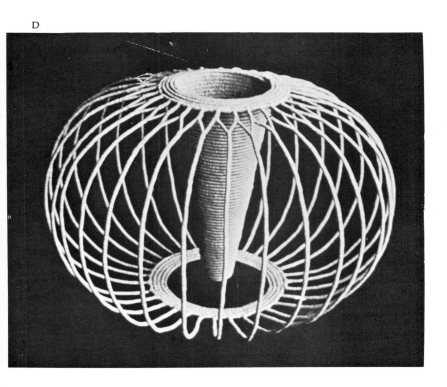

A

A
Hisako Sekijima
UNTITLED
Twined (tee twining open work); willow, rattan; 13¾ inches in diameter, 4½ inches high. Photo by Bob Hanson.

Basketmaking is, in one sense, my confirmation of the possibility to adjust the cycle of human life to the cycle of nature, just as much as to keep in our mind the significant fact that we are a part of nature. It is a clue to consider the relationship of human hands and the materials from nature.

B
Patti Lechman
PAWLEY'S BASKET
Knotted with crocheted interior; waxed nylon; 2½ by 3 by 2½ inches.

My forms are not baskets as much as they are statements about baskets. They are containers for space and for spirits, not intended to be used to carry and to store things. They function as exuberant expressions of form, texture and color.

C
Michele Hament
PINE NEEDLE BASKET WITH FEATHERS
Coiled (openwork coiling); dyed pine needles, raffia, pheasant feathers; 8½ by 8 inches.

B

C

A

Carole Stolte
PINES OF VARIED KINDS
Coiled; pine needles,
porcupine quills; 6 by 6
by 4½ inches.

*It was interesting to work with
such similar materials from
two different kingdoms: one
plant, one animal . . . interesting - but painful.*

B

Hisako Sekijima
UNTITLED
Twined; cherry bark,
raffia, linen, maple splint;
9 by 8 by 5 inches. Photo
by Shohei Matsufuji.

C

Jane Sauer
RELATIONSHIPS I
Knotted waxed linen
with ends painted; 4 by
8½ by 4 inches and 5½
by 11½ by 5½ inches.
Photo by Huntley Barad.

D

Shereen LaPlantz
UNTITLED
Plaited, sewn; flat paper
fiber splint, lauhala,
waxed linen; 10 by 11 by
10 inches.

E

Michele Hament
WILLOW STILT BASKET
Plaited, inkle loom woven
strips; cotton, willow,
waxed linen, feathers; 4
by 10 by 6 inches.

A

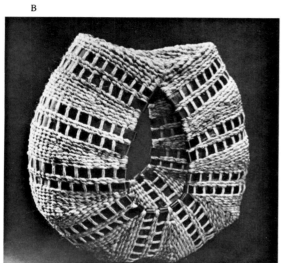

B

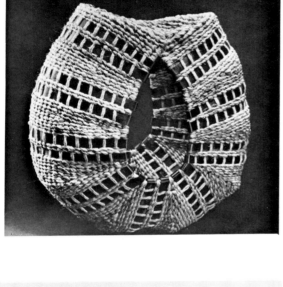

C

D

E

A

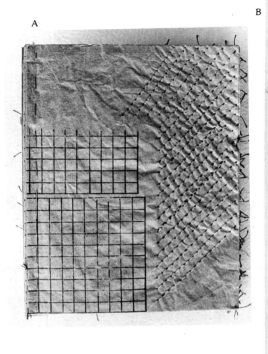

B

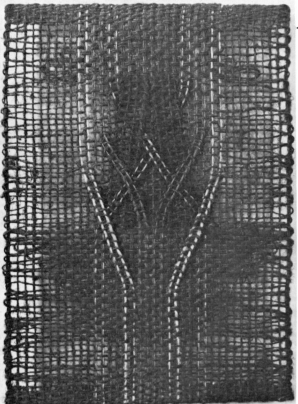

A
Suellen Glashausser
BLUE/RED GRID BOOK
Stitched; used paper, silk
thread, rubber stamping;
7 by 9 inches.

B
Elizabeth Tsuk
UNTITLED
Plain woven, low warp,
extra warps in central
area woven in relief;
linen; 6 by 9 inches.

C
D. R. Wagner
FIVE GAITED HORSES
Needle-made tapestry,
625 stitches per square
inch; cotton floss on
cotton canvas; 10¾ by 8
inches. Photo by
Hollmarc Prods.

D
D. R. Wagner
PUGS IN PARADISE
Needle-made tapestry,
625 stitches per square
inch; cotton floss on
cotton canvas; 6 by 4
inches. Photo by
Hollmarc Prods.

E
Anne Tenenbaum
TROPICS
Appliqued, embroidered,
painted collage; cotton
fabric, copper, fabric
dye, acrylic, gesso; 11 by
12 inches. Photo by John
Mann.

C

E

D

Rosalind Claire
FLYING CHERUBS
Natural cotton with hand
painted heads, satin
wings; life size.

A

B

C

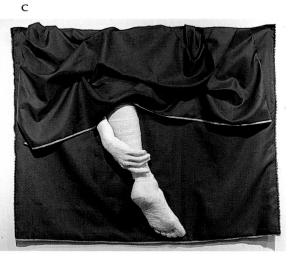

A

Lynn S. Hall
VANITAS
Soft sculpture; wool
roving, stretch tights,
synthetic fabrics, acrylic
paint, wood and wire
armature, mirror; 41 by
35 by 26 inches.

B

Barbara Simon
TOWELS ON TILE
Woven linen tiles,
chenille towels, silk and
pearl cotton soap; 22 by
14 by 4 inches.

C

Margaret Sherman
LEG ON PURPLE
Sculptural banner;
plaster, gauze, polyester;
34½ by 29½ by 3 inches.

D

Lynn S. Hall
COCKTAIL PARTY
Soft sculpture; wool
roving, stretch tights,
synthetic fabrics, acrylic
paint, wood and wire
armature, fur, feathers;
42 by 41 by 28 inches.

COCKTAIL PARTY *is a
satirical work drawn from my
childhood. Having grown up
in the rarefied atmosphere of
country clubs, I am intrigued
by the decadent and ridiculous
side of the upper-class world.*

D

A
Michael Kashey
THE LUTE PLAYER
Hand and machine stitched, quilted; cotton velveteen, beads, feathers, braid, papier-mache; 10 by 23 by 11 inches.

Exploration of time and space in dealing with the quiet moments of man's existence is the essence of my work. With the use of fine, elegant fabrics and materials, along with the knowledge of traditional fiber working techniques, I hope to create a costumed figure that is epigrammatic of man's existence.

B
Carol Burton Burns (Hunter)
JESTER
Machine and hand stitched body with crocheted and knitted leg warmers, head and hands are carved wood; antique fabrics, leather shoes, ribbons, bells; 25 by 13½ by 17 inches.

My work is greatly influenced by the primitive or folk artists who imaginatively utilize a wide range of materials and techniques. In keeping with the folk art tradition, my materials are gleaned from my environment and are seldom purchased in a store. The value of these materials that give the power of life-forces to my sculpture is immeasurable.

C
Lois Schklar
SOFT JUMPING JACK
Quilted body, sculpted face, dyed, stitched; silk, upholstery material, dye, lace, buttons; 8 by 20 by 3 inches.

A

B

C

A

A
Janice St. Croix
CAROUSEL
Needlepointed on canvas;
Persian yarn, balsa wood,
metallic yarn, mirrors,
motor and lights; 15 by
14 by 17 inches.

*The design of this carousel was
based on a composite of
carousels that were operating
in the early 1900's. The
needlepoint covers a balsa wood
base. A motor and lights were
added for the enjoyment of
children.*

B
Sonja Saar
JOE
Handknitted and cro-
cheted; wool, synthetics;
36 inches tall.

B

A
Annie Dempsey
LIKE THE BIRDS IN
A TREE . . .
Crocheted (reinforced);
pearl cotton, camel hair;
18 by 10 by 3 inches.

B
Camrose Ducote
MANDRILL
Sculpture constructed of
chicken wire, covered
with fiberfill, fabric,
paint; 21 by 16 by 20
inches. Photo by Frank
A. Ducote.

C
Andrea V. Uravitch
MOO COW: A DEDICATION
TO MOTHERHOOD
Crocheted over wooden
and foam rubber base;
wool, glass eyes, cloth; 53
by 37½ by 16 inches.
Photo by Andrea V.
Uravitch.

A

B

C

A

B

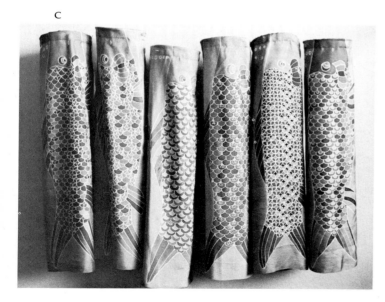

C

D

A
Susan J. Parks
SNOWBIRD
Resist dyed; silk, cedar
frame; 5 by 4 feet.

B
Martha Gibson
THE VAGABOND
Hand painted, photo-
screened printed images;
aniline and fiber reactive
dyes, silk satin with a
collapsible wooden dowel
frame; 72 by 50 by 36
inches.

C
Carol Lowell
WINDSOCKS
Hand painted; silk, dye,
gutta resist, wire hoops;
5 inch diameter, 23
inches tall.

D
Teresa Nomura
WATERFALL WIND
SCULPTURE
Nylon, aluminum poles,
nylon rope; 6 by 15 by 55
feet.

A
Donna M. Hill-Chaney
TUXEDO TAILS/
FORMAL FLIGHT
Machine and hand
stitched; cotton, satin,
lace, buttons; 18 by 14 by
16 inches.

B
Pamela Perry
WATER FAN
Woven, interlocking warp
and weft; hand dyed
cotton and linen,
feathers, pear wood; 17
by 14 inches. Photo by
David Caras.

*I prefer small, intimate objects
that use shaped textiles in
intricate ways. Fans solve this
in a way that is also
functional. I hope my work
resembles something lost or left
behind by elves or fairies as
their world of magic intrigues
me.*

C
Connie Miller
PEACH SLICE
Handmade paper; cotton,
raffia, bamboo; 34 by 24
inches.

D
Emily Reece
FEMININE RITUAL FAN II
Appliqued, quilted,
embroidered, painted
fabric assemblage;
embroidery floss, satin,
lace from a crinoline,
garters, rhinestones; 19½
by 10¼ inches.

*My art speaks of my life
experiences as a woman - in
fantasy and in reality. I incorporate objects which connect
the viewer with the object seen
in a new context.*

A
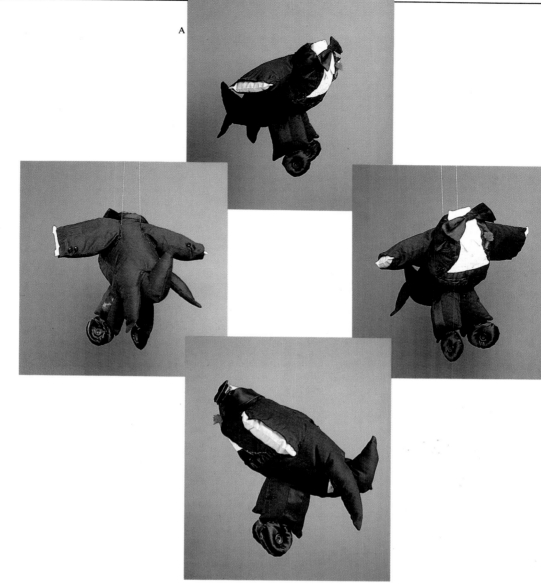

B
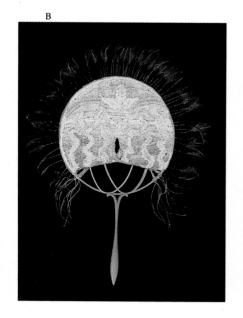

C

D
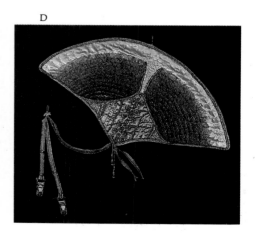

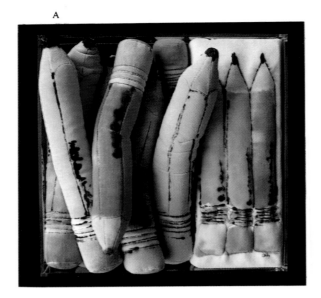

A

B

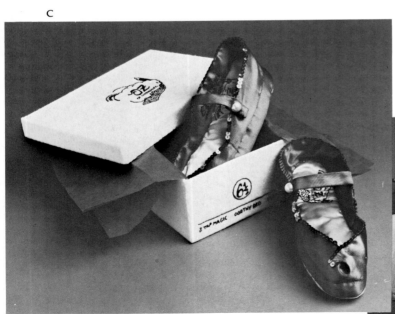

C

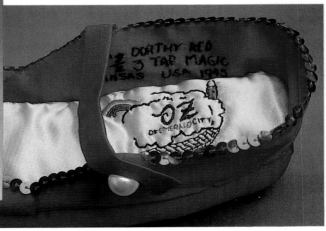

A
Cindy Hickok
PENCIL BOX
Fiber reactive dye, cotton velveteen, polyester fiberfill, plexiglass box; 12 by 12 by 2 inches.

B
Jennifer Bennett
BATHMAT
Woven tapestry; cotton warp, wool weft; 24 by 20 inches.
This piece is now in use as a bathmat in a home in Vancouver, B.C., Canada.

C
Donna M. Hill-Chaney
MAGICAL RUBY SLIPPERS
Hand stitched, embroidered; satin, felt, cardboard shoe box, sequins, real buttons; box - 4 by 11¼ by 7 inches, shoes - 3 by 10 by 4 inches.
This work was produced especially for a "Wizard of Oz" Exhibition.

A
Jappie King Black
FLYING SIREN
Crocheted, stitched,
wrapped, hand painted;
cotton, linen, silk, wool,
alpaca, paper rush; 24 by
14 by 22 inches. Photo by
Richard W. Black.

*FLYING SIREN is the second
in a series of bird ladies. The
siren is a creature from the
ancient Greek myth, the story
of Jason and the Argonauts.
She is a temptress, half
woman/half bird, luring
sailors into dangerous waters
by singing sweetly. This piece
is in flight.*

B
Susanna E. Lewis
FOUR FIGURES
Machine knitted, stuffed,
shaped; cotton yarn,
polyester stuffing; 7½
inches in diameter, 3½
inches tall each.

C
Genevieve P. Lykes
SCHOOL OF FISH
Dyed fiber and plexiglass
construction; cotton,
dyed gauze; 24 by 24 by
8 inches. Photo by
Surfside Three.

D
Jan Manley
MONKEY BAG
Hand and machine
stitched, appliqued,
braided handle; polished
cotton, embroidery floss,
silk lined; 8 by 10 by 4
inches. Photo by Jan
Manley.

A

B

C

D

THE FIBERARTS DESIGN BOOK II

EDITOR:
Jeane Hutchins

ART DIRECTOR:
Steve Millard

TYPESETTER:
Elaine Thompson

PRODUCTION MANAGER:
Nancy Ward

BUSINESS MANAGER:
Kate Pulleyn

PUBLISHER:
Rob Pulleyn

TECHNICAL ADVISOR:
Rich Mathews

EDITORIAL ASSISTANTS:
Pat Wald, Joy Weeber

COLOR SEPARATIONS:
World Color (cover), Colourscan

PAPER:
Art Paper 80 lb.

TYPEFACE:
Andover 8 pt.

FIBERARTS MAGAZINE

EDITOR:
Chris Timmons

PUBLISHER:
Rob Pulleyn

STAFF:
Henry Barrett, Vicky Bay, Jeff Britton, Jill Casey, Hervey Evans, Rick Frizzell, Judy Godfrey, Jeane Hutchins, Steve Millard, Fleta Monaghan, Kate Pulleyn, Dennis Swinehart, Elaine Thompson, Pat Wald, Nancy Ward.

INDEX